"Learning to treat yourself with kindness and compassion is like learning to place your feet firmly on the ground. If you are going to walk out of your struggle with anxiety, you need to regain your psychological footing, and this book will show you how. In a gentle, wise, and step-by-step way, it will help you establish self-compassion as a habit of mind and bring that healing quality to your thoughts and actions. Highly recommended."

—Steven C. Hayes, PhD, author of *Get Out of Your Mind and Into Your Life*

"Easy to read, grounded in solid research, and filled with useful exercises, this book is a godsend for those who suffer from anxiety."

—Kristin Neff, PhD, associate professor at the University of Texas at Austin and author of *Self-Compassion*

"Cognitive behavior therapy (CBT) has led the way in creating solid science-based treatments. Traditionally, CBT has been an action-oriented treatment, and that action orientation has produced a lot of benefits. More recently, CBT has begun to include more work focused on acceptance, mindfulness, and self-compassion. Dennis Tirch is a master of where CBT has been and of where CBT is going. In this book, you will find a broad contemporary understanding of anxiety and a host of very, very practical ways to come into a more compassionate relationship with anxiety. The book offers a different way of being with anxiety that will have implications in your life that extend well beyond anxiety. You can expect changes in your relationship with anxiety that offer a path to rich and engaged living."

—Kelly G. Wilson, PhD, cofounder of acceptance and commitment therapy, associate professor at the University of Mississippi, and author of *Things Might Go Terribly, Horribly Wrong*

"Tirch writes with warmth and wisdom, as if he is speaking directly to you. He shows how compassion, mindfulness, and facing the difficulties of anxiety can bring personal growth. Filled with specific and powerful techniques, readers will find a new path to follow with a brilliant and compassionate guide. I highly recommend this book for all who suffer from anxiety."

—Robert L. Leahy, PhD, director of The American Institute for Cognitive Therapy , clinical professor of psychology at Weill-Cornell University Medical College, and author of *The Worry Cure*

"A superb introduction to a revolutionary new way of dealing with anxiety. The reader is led on a compelling exploration of how the anxious mind works, followed by masterful exercises that tap our innate capacity for comfort and healing self-compassion. Seamlessly integrating important research and extensive clinical experience, the author speaks through the pages with the wise, gentle voice of experience. Go ahead, try it and see what happens!"

—Christopher K. Germer, PhD, clinical instructor at Harvard Medical School and author of *The Mindful Path to Self-Compassion*

"Writing in an informative, highly engaging manner, Tirch shares his considerable wisdom in both compassion-based practices and behavior therapy. He gives the reader practical and powerful tools for cultivating a sense of self-compassion in the face of anxiety. A genuine pleasure to read."

—Douglas Mennin, associate professor at Hunter College of The City University of New York

"*The Compassionate-Mind Guide to Overcoming Anxiety* is one of the most practical and accessible books for living a meaningful life despite the presence of anxiety, panic, and worry. Expect to feel compelled toward action immediately."

—Todd B. Kashdan, PhD, associate professor of psychology at George Mason University and author of *Curious? Discover the Missing Ingredient to a Fulfilling Life*

"The Compassionate-Mind Guide to Overcoming Anxiety is a remarkable integration of modern science and seasoned wisdom. Tirch's accessible writing style draws you into learning about overcoming anxiety. He even weaves beer and cake, purple gorillas, and ten-thousand-year-old poems into his writing to help you embrace a richer understanding of the anxiety and compassion connection."

—D.J. Moran, PhD, author of ACT in Practice

"The Compassionate-Mind Guide to Overcoming Anxiety thoughtfully addresses the experience of anxiety and is written with obvious care for the person who suffers from anxiety. Tirch's personal style and client examples bring the book to life. This is an easy-to-understand read that paves a path to self-compassion that is engaging and wise."

—Robyn D. Walser, PhD, coauthor of The Mindful Couple

"This book is an excellent resource for individuals suffering from anxiety. Using step-by-step strategies, Tirch systematically guides people to the invaluable tools they need to overcome their suffering and build a life filled with meaning. With wisdom and clarity, he shows how one can use compassion and mindfulness to face anxiety and bring about a fundamental life change. This book is truly a pleasure to read and will be an invaluable guide for anxiety sufferers."

—Lata K. McGinn, PhD, coauthor of Treatment of Obsessive Compulsive Disorder and Treatment Plans and Interventions for Anxiety and Depression

THE COMPASSIONATE-MIND GUIDE TO

OVERCOMING ANXIETY

using compassion-focused therapy to calm worry, panic, and fear

DENNIS D. TIRCH, PHD

New Harbinger Publications, Inc.

Publisher's Note

This publication is designed to provide accurate and authoritative information in regard to the subject matter covered. It is sold with the understanding that the publisher is not engaged in rendering psychological, financial, legal, or other professional services. If expert assistance or counseling is needed, the services of a competent professional should be sought.

Distributed in Canada by Raincoast Books

Copyright © 2012 by Dennis D. Tirch
New Harbinger Publications, Inc.
5674 Shattuck Avenue
Oakland, CA 94609
www.newharbinger.com

Acquired by Tesilya Hanauer; Cover design by Amy Shoup;
Edited by Carole Honeychurch; Text design by Tracy Carlson

Library of Congress Cataloging-in-Publication Data

Tirch, Dennis D., 1968-
  The compassionate-mind guide to overcoming anxiety : using compassion-focused
therapy to calm worry, panic, and fear / Dennis Tirch ; foreword by Paul Gilbert.
      p. cm.
  Includes bibliographical references.
  ISBN 978-1-60882-036-8 (pbk. : alk. paper)
  1. Anxiety. 2. Emotion-focused therapy. I. Title.
  BF575.A6T57 2012
  152.4'6--dc23

                                        2012005438

Printed in the United States of America

12 11 10   10 9 8 7 6 5 4 3 2 1   First printing

To my mother, Janet

Contents

PART I

The Compassionate Mind Approach to Overcoming Anxiety

1

PART II
Compassionate Mind Training for Anxiety

6

• Mindfulness • Directly Learning about Attention • Reflecting on
Your First Mindfulness Practice • How to Practice • Where to
Practice • When to Practice • Further Mindfulness Exercises
• Challenges on the Path to Mindfulness and Compassion

7

• The Power of the Imagination • The Roots of Imagery • Six
Imagery Exercises • Using Compassionate Imagery in Everyday Life

8

• Moving from the Anxious Mind toward Compassionate Thinking
• Bringing Compassionate Thinking Closer into Contact with Worries
and Anxious Thoughts • Techniques for Engaging Compassionate
Thinking • Compassionate Responding • Distinguishing
Self-Criticism from Compassionate Self-Correction
• Compassionate Defusion

9

• Why Bother? Clarifying Your Goals and Valued Aims • Gradually
Developing Compassionate Behavior • Self-Compassion in Action
• Reflecting on Your Valued Aims and Planning for Compassionate
Behavior • Developing the Motivation to Face Your Fears • Exposure
on a Gradual, Compassionate Path • Taking Compassionate Exposure
Further and Facing Fear in Everyday Life

10

Moving Forward with Compassion and
"Beginning Again, Constantly"

Preface

When we experience disappointment, fear, or loss, we naturally tend to look for support and guidance from those we care about and who care about us. We turn to them for their acceptance, their understanding, and their love. Indeed, the evolution of human behavior demonstrates how this tendency has emerged in the life cycle and how we've become able to keenly detect threats in our environment while at the same time abiding in a state of calm through our experience of the support and loving-kindness of those around us. Research has shown that, from the day we're born and throughout our lives, the kindness of others will have a huge impact on how our brains mature, on how our bodies work, and on our emotions and general well-being.[1] It has also been shown that treating ourselves with compassion has a huge impact on the quality of our lives and how we deal with difficulties, such as anxiety.[2]

It makes sense that we're calmed by a connection to people who are warm and compassionate toward us. It also makes sense that we can develop healthier ways of responding to life's struggles by directing compassion and kindness inward, to the way we feel about ourselves.

Our lives can feel so overwhelming and can be so very short. In the presence of a variety of fearful challenges along our journeys, such as sickness, aging, and the finitude of life, can we direct accepting, open, and warm feelings toward ourselves? If we're capable of such acts, what's their effect? By standing as a compassionate witness to our own pain, can we better be present to our experience and develop healthier, more fluid ways of responding to life's struggles? This "self-compassion" may be the foundation for a more flexible, healthy, and rewarding life.[3] This book aims to help you understand the nature of your anxiety, the best ways of dealing with it, and how your mind can help you cope with it.

Foreword

We have always understood that compassion is very important for our well-being. If you are feeling stressed or upset, it is always better to have kind, helpful, and supportive people around you rather than critical, rejecting, or disinterested folk. It is not only common sense, however, that tells us about the value of kindness and compassion—recent advances in the scientific study of compassion and kindness have greatly advanced our understanding of how compassionate qualities of the mind really do influence our brains, bodies, and social relationships, as well as affect our health and well-being. Yet despite this ancient commonsense wisdom and new knowledge, we live in an age that can make compassion for ourselves and others problematic. This is a world of striving for the competitive edge, of achievement and desire, of comparison to others who are perhaps doing better than we are, leading to dissatisfaction and self-criticism. Research has now revealed that such environments actually make us unhappier and that mental ill health is on the increase, especially in younger people. As Dennis Tirch helps us understand, anxiety is a very common symptom of the environments we are living in today.

As if feeling anxious and stressed were not enough, we can also become fearful of these emotions and try to suppress or avoid them, even becoming self-critical for feeling overly anxious. Indeed, our society has a habit of blaming and shaming if we seem to be struggling with our emotions. People with "the right stuff" are not supposed to be anxious or feel overwhelmed. So anxiety must be an indication that there is something wrong with us. Rather than seeing it as an understandable, if undesirable, response to the world in which we live, we blame ourselves for feeling anxious.

So, why are we so susceptible to anxiety, and why might anxiety be on the increase in modern society? Dr. Tirch uses his wealth of experience and knowledge to guide our understanding and help us recognize that actually many of our emotions are the result of a very long evolutionary history. Our emotions were originally developed to help us deal with rapidly approaching threats in the jungles and savannas and are not so well adapted for the modern world. Nor do they do so well when we bring our advanced brains and greater capacity for thinking and rumination to bear on our anxiety. Humans are the only animals that have the ability to worry about tomorrow, or whether they have cancer, or whether they're about to have a heart attack, or whether they're liked. So the way we think about the stresses in our lives can at times really "do our heads in." And, of course, we can also think about our internal worlds—the fantasies, thoughts, and feelings we have within us. Again, no other animal can do this. Realizing this and being able to stand back from it all allows us to understand that our vulnerability to anxiety is not our fault. After all, we didn't design our brains, with their various capacities for such emotions as anxiety and anger. Nor did we design our brains' capacity for complex thinking, which can actually make our experience of anxiety more intense. And we didn't choose our backgrounds or our genes, both of which can make us more susceptible to anxiety. This is a very important message in compassionate mind training and compassion-focused therapy, because compassion begins with a deep understanding of just how tricky our brains are and a recognition that they are not that well put together! Once we recognize how difficult our emotions can be, we can stand back from them and feel compassion for the difficulties we experience.

So, given that our brains have evolved in and been shaped by the environments we live in, what can we do to help ourselves when we become anxious? First, we can learn to pay attention to how our minds work and function, becoming mindful and observant of the feelings that are associated with anxiety. In this very helpful book, Dr. Tirch shows how people have learned to be sensitive to feelings of anxiety and, at times, have also learned to be frightened of those feelings.

If we are to face anxiety and work with it, then our relationship with ourselves is very important. If we are critical and harsh with ourselves, then our inner worlds are not comfortable places to inhabit. Feeling ashamed and being self-critical, self-condemning, or even self-loathing can undermine our confidence and make us feel bad. Sadly, when things go wrong and we make mistakes, many of us are self-critical rather than helpful and supportive of ourselves, and when we feel distressed we react by becoming frustrated and angry. This is not, in fact, a good way to deal with anxiety because, as Dr. Tirch outlines, you are actually adding more fuel to the fire of your threat-detection system. In contrast, self-compassion is a way of being with ourselves in all our emotions, uncomfortable as they may be, without self-condemnation and instead with support and encouragement. Research shows that the more compassionate we are toward ourselves, the happier we are and the more resilient we become when faced with difficult events in our lives. In addition, we are better able to reach out to others for help, and we feel more compassionate toward other people, too.

Compassion is sometimes viewed as being a bit "soft" or "weak" or "letting your guard down" and "not trying hard enough." This is a major mistake because, on the contrary, compassion requires us to be open to and tolerant of our painful feelings and to face up to our own problematic emotions and difficulties. Compassion does not mean turning away from emotional difficulties or discomforts or trying to get rid of them. It is *not* a soft option. Rather, compassion provides us with the courage, honesty, and commitment to learn to cope with the difficulties we face, and it alleviates our anxiety. It enables us to do things that help us to flourish and take care of ourselves—not as a demand or requirement, but to enable us to live our lives more fully and contentedly.

In this book, Dr. Tirch offers his many years of experience as a clinical psychologist, psychotherapist, and longtime meditator working in New York with people experiencing a variety of emotional difficulties. He also brings his experience of using compassion-focused therapy in the treatment of anxiety. He outlines a model of compassion that seeks to stimulate and build your confidence so that you can engage with your anxiety. You will learn how to develop a real, supportive friendship with yourself that will help you through difficult times. Dr. Tirch guides you to develop compassionate motivations, compassionate attention, compassionate feelings, compassionate thinking, and compassionate behavior. You will learn about the potential power of developing compassionate imagery that focuses on creating a compassionate sense of yourself and that draws on your own inner wisdom and benevolent qualities—qualities you are most likely to feel when you're feeling calm and/or showing concern for others. Learning how to breathe, to "slow down," and also to engage with these qualities can be very helpful when anxiety crashes through you like a storm. Using different compassionate images, you will discover that your compassion focus can be visual or aural (e.g., imagining a compassionate voice speaking to you when you need it) and can be especially useful in enabling you to get in touch with your internal compassionate feelings and desires at times of distress.

The approach that Dr. Tirch takes is called a compassionate *mind* approach because when we engage compassion it can influence our attention, thoughts, feelings, and behavior—in other words, how our mind operates *as a whole*. The compassionate mind approach outlined in this book draws on many other well-developed approaches, including those of Eastern traditions such as Buddhism. In addition, compassionate mind approaches, especially those that form part of compassion-focused therapy, are rooted in scientific understanding of the working of the mind. Undoubtedly over the years our understanding of the brain will change and advance. One thing that doesn't change, however, is the fact that kindness, warmth, and understanding go a long way toward helping us. In these pages you will find these qualities in abundance so you, too, can learn to be gentle, understanding, supportive, and kind, but also engaging and courageous, when working with your anxiety.

Many people suffer silently and secretly with a whole range of anxiety problems—some feel ashamed or angry with themselves, and others are sometimes fearful that their anxiety will get the upper hand. Sadly, shame stops many of us from reaching out for help. But, by opening your heart to compassion, you can take the first steps toward dealing with your anxieties in new ways. My compassionate wishes go with you on your journey.

—Professor Paul Gilbert, PhD, FBPsS, OBE
August 2011

A Personal Story and Acknowledgments

Before we go further, let me share with you how this book came into being. As it happens, my personal connection to training in mindfulness, acceptance, and compassion began long before I became a psychologist. As a child, at about the age of ten, I was lucky enough to learn the basics of Buddhist meditation from an uncle who'd served as a paratrooper in the Second World War. He discovered that Zen Buddhism helped him cope with the harrowing experiences he'd had. I suppose he must have noticed how anxious and curious I was, and he began to teach me *zazen*, a form of Japanese meditation that relates to the practice of mindfulness, which is a way of staying in the present moment as deliberately and as fully as possible and partly involves paying attention to your breathing, moment by moment. I noticed that even when my uncle recalled the sadness and insanity of his wartime experience, his face was graced with a slight smile and he seemed to be full of love and kindness. It impressed me so much that I started on the path that leads to the book you're holding.

In my early twenties, after completing a degree in philosophy and humanities, my attention again turned to an understanding of how Buddhist thought and mind-training exercises could help alleviate suffering. These were the days before "mindfulness" and "acceptance" had become trendy terms in Western psychotherapy. My own meditative practice and studies led me to wonder how mindfulness and compassion could be skillfully applied in a modern, Western context. I had no idea how to accomplish this.

After a fair amount of soul-searching, I enrolled in graduate school to study psychology. Eventually, I began a PhD course in clinical psychology, with a vision of integrating what I'd learned from Buddhist mental training with state-of-the-art Western psychology. I soon realized that the most exciting and effective research and clinical work in psychotherapy were happening at the cutting edge of cognitive behavioral therapy (CBT), which was emerging as a major, effective therapy for a range of difficulties including anxiety. I spent a great deal of time cross-referencing CBT principles with those found in Mahayana Buddhism and envisioning an effective, practical therapy that would use both methods.

On the horizon, and about to enter the field of CBT, other psychologists were starting to explore adaptations of Buddhist contemplative thought as alternative forms of behavior therapy. Throughout the 1990s a psychologist named Steven Hayes and a number of his colleagues were developing acceptance and commitment therapy (ACT),[1] which involved learning to accept thoughts and emotions as they arise and living in accordance with our deepest values. Marsha Linehan, a psychologist and student of Zen Buddhism, developed dialectical behavior therapy (DBT)[2] for people with turbulent emotions who might be prone to suicide attempts. Both ACT and DBT merged Eastern and Western psychologies and amassed a strong body of research that provided a sound base of evidence for their effectiveness.

When I was at graduate school, something else happened that profoundly affected me: my father died from diabetes. The disease caused his death to be slow, and the process was regrettably difficult for him; however, during his illness I was able to visit him while he was in the hospital. He was always dignified during this time, and he talked to me of many things, including his guilt over things he'd done, or not done, and his pain. He was also hoping for some kind of redemption or absolution before his life ended, and he was filled with anxiety. He needed compassion, and I felt it was one of the most important things, indeed perhaps the only thing, I'd be able to give him. This experience, however dreadful and sad, allowed me to understand the way compassion could bring peace, restfulness, and calm to a worried, anxious mind.

During my internship and postdoctoral training, two factors brought me into much closer contact with the power of acceptance, compassion, and applied mindfulness. Mindfulness can be understood as nonjudgmental observation of the contents of our consciousness. Compassion and mindfulness work hand in hand to help us develop a nonjudgmental awareness of ourselves. As we work with our habitual tendency to judge our thoughts and feelings, we're working toward the development of mindfulness, which in turn helps us cultivate self-compassion. Mindfulness and compassion are related but separate processes. But of the two factors that brought me close to the practice of mindfulness, the first was personal: I spent many hours walking through the green, rural campus of the Bedford (Massachusetts) Veterans Affairs Medical Center with our training director, Richard Amodio, discussing a variety of ways that mindfulness and compassion could be used in psychotherapy. As a result, we designed and piloted a group treatment for Vietnam-era veterans with heavy combat trauma. This pilot program brought us into contact with clients who taught us a great deal about the power of compassion and self-forgiveness, and I believe we were all changed through the process of treatment.

The second factor to influence me was the absolute explosion in research and publishing involving CBT and mindfulness. The field of study we were involved with seemed to change and expand each week. As a result, I immersed myself in the academic literature; what I learned transformed my life's work and ultimately led me to the practice of compassion-focused therapy (CFT), on which this book is based.

For the past nine years I've worked with Robert Leahy at the American Institute for Cognitive Therapy, where I serve as associate director. Our institute is an internationally known CBT practice and a center of training for psychology graduate students, professionals, and postdoctoral residents. Dr. Leahy is a well-known master clinician and a prolific writer in the field of CBT; he has a broad perspective that takes in a range of psychological insights and discoveries. Over several years, Dr. Leahy and I have been engaged in an active research program to examine the relationships between people's beliefs about their emotions and their capacity for mindfulness and acceptance, as well as for many other variables.[3]

I've been fortunate to attend a number of residential and intensive trainings led by such teachers as Steven Hayes, Kelly Wilson, Zindel Segal, Chris Germer, and Robyn Walser. I'm also grateful to have been involved in the development of a growing ACT community in New York City. We've been steadily developing new opportunities for therapists who are seeking training in mindfulness and acceptance–based therapy. During this time, my consultation with Kelly Wilson has been particularly important to developing an understanding of how fundamental behavioral processes can unfold into the awe-inspiring human capacity for compassion.

Along with this scientific study, some of my most profound lessons have taken place in spiritual contexts, such as my ongoing work with Buddhist and Central Asian meditation traditions, and on extended music and meditation retreats led by the English guitarist Robert Fripp. Currently, my personal spiritual studies have returned to Zen, yoga, and Tibetan Buddhism; however, I've found that all forms of meditative and psychotherapy practice I've encountered have had their usefulness. There are certain principles regarding how we can interact with our inner selves and the world around us in ways that contribute to our well-being. At the heart of these principles, again and again, is the importance of compassion.

In the middle of this activity, some six years ago, Dr. Leahy introduced me to Professor Paul Gilbert, a good friend of his. This introduction radically affected my professional and personal life; Professor Gilbert is a master of the topics of evolutionary psychology and the neuroscience of emotion and is also deeply involved in exploring how Buddhist concepts, such as compassion and mindfulness, can be used outside the bounds of strictly spiritual settings and linked to modern psychological science. He has done a great deal of work on shame and self-criticism and has found that people who are prone to feeling shameful and critical of themselves also have a hard time being open to the compassion of others and to the idea of developing self-compassion,[4] which they see as a weakness or even something to be frightened of. So, compassion, and especially developing self-compassion, became a key focus for his work, because evidence was pointing to the fact that our brains work much more efficiently and are much more able to remain on an even keel if we surround ourselves with people who are kind, supportive, and compassionate.[5]

When I began to read Paul's work, I had the sense that many threads of my professional life were being woven together in his new approach: compassion-focused therapy (CFT), which builds on the insights and developments of a variety of fields in psychotherapy but in particular on CBT. It draws on what research is telling us about how our brains process emotion and the way our brains have evolved to require certain social inputs, and it draws on Eastern psychology's history of mind training. Paul believes, as I do, that before you can fix something you need to know how it works, and that can come only from the science. We began to correspond and collaborate, and for a number of subsequent years CFT became a central aspect of my own clinical work, research, and writing.

After we worked on a chapter and an article together, I visited Paul in Derby in the United Kingdom to take part in his training and to discuss CFT in greater depth. I was accompanied by Russell Kolts, who's now studying and writing about how compassionate mind training can help patients overcome problems with anger and uncontrollable rage. I was fascinated by the possibilities that CFT provided, and the time spent with Paul and Russell again broadened my perspective to the humbling, healing power of mindful compassion. It was when I was with them that the idea for this book emerged. I've been very lucky to build a relationship with Paul and with Russell, who've fueled my dedication to this work.

I'd like to acknowledge Kristin Neff and Christopher Germer for the groundbreaking work they've conducted on self-compassion, as well as Lynne Henderson, Chris Irons, and Kenn Goss for the significant advances they've made in applications of CFT. These folks are part of a growing community within psychological science that understands the importance of compassion to our well-being. Of course, I'm deeply grateful for the help of the editors of this book, Professor Paul Gilbert and Fritha Saunders. I'd also like to take a moment to recognize the wisdom and compassion that I've learned from clients, close colleagues such as Dr Laura Silberstein, students, and my family—John, Leah, Lily, Neal, and Jaclyn—as well as my mother, Janet, truly my first teacher in compassion.

HOW THIS BOOK IS STRUCTURED

Given that you're holding this book, it's likely you've had some trouble with anxiety at some point in your life. My hope is that the practices I describe will open the way to greater self-compassion, well-being, and a growing capacity to bring mindful awareness and kindness into your life, moment by moment.

It may be useful for you to have a pen and paper or special notebook nearby so that you can record any observations you may have as you read this book and so that you can complete or copy some of the exercises.

This book is divided into two parts: part I provides background information that explores the evolutionary nature of anxiety and how it operates. Part II examines how we're able to soothe our anxiety by experiencing a sense of safety, contentment, and calm. You'll learn of the sometimes-untapped capacities we have to alleviate our anxiety using our intuitive wisdom, courage, and compassion. Part II also provides detailed, workable, and user-friendly techniques based on CFT to help you overcome your anxiety. The most significant techniques in this section are called compassionate mind training; they aim to help you balance the way you regulate your emotions and in particular (but not exclusively) stimulate the system in your brain that helps you feel safe and connected (what we call "affiliated") with others and with your own compassionate self.

CFT uses imagery and visualization techniques adapted from Buddhist practices as well as modern CBT techniques. It's deeply important that, during this process, you imagine having a very good friend with you—one who cares completely about you and wants to see you prosper.

In CFT we talk a lot about building the capacity for compassion, to prepare you for the work ahead. If you want to run a marathon you should train for it gradually and deliberately, rather than simply attempt it one day. Developing the ability to accept, regulate, and cope with anxiety follows a similar course of training.

The aim of part II is to provide a practical, reliable, and repeatable program to help you develop a compassionate mind when you feel anxious or distressed.

—Dennis Tirch, 2011

PART I

The Compassionate Mind Approach to Overcoming Anxiety

1

The Emergence of Anxiety

Anxiety is one of the most common problems that people face. Many rather ordinary activities may provoke anxiety: applying for a job, taking an exam, meeting new people. There's potential for anxiety in almost everything around us. You won't be surprised when I tell you that working as a cognitive behavioral psychotherapist in the heart of midtown Manhattan, I've spent a lot of time in the presence of a wide variety of types of anxiety. Manhattan is one of those busy metropolitan cities that can seem obsessed with getting things done, and it's crowded with people hurrying along the streets. It's easy to imagine the almost mythical promise of opportunity, laced with the experience of lightning-paced stress, linked to expectations and deadlines. Just outside my window, the pavement is heaving with people rushing around in pursuit of their goals, many chatting or texting on their cell phones. Even if I close my eyes, the pulsing sound of the traffic, the occasional siren, the beeping horns, and the constant hum of activity reverberates through the windows and walls.

It was in this city, packed into a crowded subway car, that one of my clients—we'll call her Jennifer—first encountered the depth and intensity of her own experience of anxiety.

Jennifer was deeply committed to her work as a preschool teacher, and she'd held her heartfelt dedication to helping young children for as long as she could remember. She had high standards for herself and was a caring and conscientious person. Her students and their families were lucky to have such a teacher in their lives. As she sat on the subway one morning, with every one of her lessons carefully planned and her smart phone with her schedule in perfect order, she seemed in control of her life.

But that particular morning, as she looked around at her densely packed fellow passengers and felt the clacking and vibrating of the train, Jennifer began to feel as if it were difficult to take a deep breath. This seemed odd—and worrisome. She began to pay close attention to this strange sensation, and as she did, her chest began to feel tight and constricted.

Oh, God, she thought. *What's happening? Am I freaking out or something? Am I coming down with the flu?*

Suddenly, she felt trapped, as if the train were closing in on her, with no possibility of escape. As these thoughts began to race through her mind, she continued to frantically check for signs that she was becoming ill—or worse. She grew dizzy and began to panic. Her brow began to bead with sweat, and she told herself: *I need to get out of here! What if I can't escape? Get me out.* Startling herself, she began to cry. She covered her face, and as soon as the train reached the next stop she pushed her way through the thick cluster of other exiting passengers and ran up the stairs to the street.

As she emerged into daylight and fresh air, Jennifer was still far from her stop, and this meant that she'd certainly be late for work. Disoriented, she looked around for a taxi, but there was none to be found. She felt waves of shame and embarrassment: she didn't understand how she could have lost control so intensely, so suddenly. Worries about being fired, or at least chided in front of her colleagues for her lateness, percolated in her imagination. Stunned, she barely managed to straighten her typically perfectly pressed and professional clothes and make her way to the school. Although she felt mortified to make the call, later that day she contacted my office and sought help for what she felt was potentially crippling anxiety. I can clearly recall our first telephone chat; every word she spoke seemed steeped in fear and self-criticism. Jennifer didn't seem to be kind and understanding toward her painful experience; instead she asked herself: *How could this have happened to me when I'm so very careful and have worked so hard to be in control? What's wrong with me? Am I going crazy? Have I lost it? Can anything help?* This wasn't the first time she'd felt trapped and panicked, and the fear of there being something wrong with her and that it was out of her control seemed to spin her around in spirals of anxiety.

Over the course of a year, Jennifer and I worked together to help her deal with what proved to be severe panic attacks and chronic worries. In time, we discovered that what proved most helpful was a special kind of mental training that involved the cultivation of an open, receptive, and nonjudgmental acceptance of herself, just as she was, at each moment. We focused on her self-criticism and her sense that something was wrong with her—a feeling of some inner flaw, so common in people who struggle with anxiety. Jennifer worked as hard at her psychotherapy as she had at other aspects of her life, but this therapeutic work didn't involve striving or rushing and, oddly for her, didn't really involve her being in control. Her therapy involved deliberately adopting an attitude of loving-kindness toward herself—of being wise and understanding about her anxiety based on what she'd learned about how anxiety works. She learned to find her "inner friend," who offered support and validation in difficult circumstances. From this secure base of self-compassion, she learned how to mindfully pay attention to her present-moment experiences and how to engage in a life of meaning and purpose.

Jennifer discovered that when she was self-critical, her inner voice was often harsh, angry, and even contemptuous—no friend at all! Having this negatively imbalanced emotional sense of herself was undermining and significantly increased her experience of stress, anxiety, and shame. After all, when we're stressed, criticism—whether it comes from within or without—is only going to make us feel more stressed. There's nothing soothing, reassuring, encouraging, or supportive about self-criticism, and one of the most important elements of Jennifer's therapy was the development of her ability to recognize her critical voice as it arose. From here, she was able to learn how to respond to herself with a more supportive, encouraging, warm, and compassionate voice. As Jennifer learned, compassion isn't about weakness or some fluffy "niceness"; it's about how we develop the courage and strength to engage with, and deal with, those things that are difficult for us to do. This friendly inner voice will in turn help us pursue our most valued aims and deal with both our so-called failures *and* our successes.

In time, Jennifer found that the deep reservoir of empathy and care she'd reserved for her students was also available for herself. Self-compassion emerged as a powerful presence in her life; she learned to live with occasional feelings of anxiety and to understand that feelings of anxiety are an inevitable, and sometimes valuable, part of life. Through her regular practice of mental training, in and out of her therapy sessions, Jennifer learned to remain calm when in the storm of anxious thoughts and feelings that sometimes moved through her mind and body.

For example, if she had to lead her class in front of the school administrator and an outside evaluator, she'd often become physically anxious and experience tension and shortness of breath before the class began. Her mind would generate all sorts of "what if" thoughts and worries: *What if I freeze? What if I don't seem confident?* But eventually Jennifer learned to divert attention from these thoughts by gently drawing attention to the present moment, by focusing on the flow of her breath into and out of her body. She learned also to focus some of her attention on the soles of her feet, so that she could feel strong and grounded by her connection to the earth; thus, she created a new way of "being with" her anxiety while still engaging in what mattered most to her: being a teacher.

Based on her training, when anxiety began to arise, Jennifer would take a moment to acknowledge her feelings and then gain perspective on the situation that was unfolding before her. In such times, Jennifer became able to remind herself of the value of her work, and she'd remind herself of her intention to help her students. If she had to lead her class under an evaluator's close and watchful eye, Jennifer would tell herself: *Teaching means so very much to me, and I want to do well and be dedicated to my students and this school. I understand that my mind is on guard against threats, given that I've always found public scrutiny pretty scary, but I know this is just a natural, human response. In this moment, I understand that it's not a fault if I feel some fear, which I can ride as if it were a wave. I can be kind to myself and do what matters most to me. I'm going to face this situation and take care of my students.* Jennifer learned to consciously surround herself with warmth, courage, and self-acceptance, and this deliberate activation of self-compassion awakened in her the instinctive emotion-regulation system that allows us to feel safe, protected, and secure in the presence of a responsive, kind, and nurturing caregiver. This provided Jennifer with just enough emotional space to engage in her lesson, despite her apprehension.

The type of mental training we worked on together is known as compassionate mind training (CMT), and this book aims to bring this training to you. Over the past several years I've worked with many clients like Jennifer who were striving intensely to be happy in a highly stressful, competitive environment. A great many of these clients have entered my consultation room and have begun their psychotherapy while suffering from debilitating levels of anxiety, which whispers worries in their minds and creates dreadful imaginary scenarios of nightmarish tomorrows. Such scenarios interrupt their moments of calm and drive up their heart rates, shorten their breath, alter the rhythm of their breathing, and may even make them feel dizzy. As a result, the joys of life and the simple pleasures of the present moment are all too often swept away in waves of anxiety and negative predictions.

THE EXPERIENCE OF ANXIETY

The word "anxiety" comes from the Latin *anxius*, which means "a feeling of agitation and upset." Today, the term "anxiety" encompasses an array of ways in which we pay attention, feel physically, and behave, and these have evolved to help us deal with possible threats in our environment.

The first way we might experience anxiety is in the way we feel physically. For example, when you last felt anxious, how did it feel to you in your body? What were your physical sensations? Did you have a tingling in your fingers? Or did your stomach tighten? Perhaps your breathing became shallow. Sometimes these physical sensations can themselves make us feel anxious—as if we become anxious about feeling anxious! When that happens, people tend to start monitoring how their bodies feel, yet their anxiety is likely to increase the more they pay attention to it.

If you were to give a one-word label to the emotion that shows up in your mind and in the way you feel physically when you feel anxious, what might it be? Fear? Anxiety? Frustration? Shame? Sadness? If so, you may understand that the brain translates the physical sensations of anxiety into a complex, uniquely human form of experience that we call emotion. Our five senses blend with memories, stories about ourselves, and our history of thoughts and beliefs to produce an emotional experience in the moment.

Imagine that you apply for a job and are selected for a five-step interview process, in which you must submit to five interviews, each with a different person. In the first four interviews, when you enter the room the interviewer looks friendly; he or she smiles and welcomes you and seems warm and curious. However, the fifth interviewer—who introduces himself as Mr. Sharcke—seems cold, and his manner is abrupt. He looks at you with dead eyes, completely expressionless. His utter lack of warmth is unnerving, and you're not sure how to read him; you sense hostility. *Mr. Scharcke*—you half wonder whether if he were to smile you'd see rows of pointy teeth.

Which of these interviews would be the one that generates the most tension and draws more of your attention? Which interview would be most on your mind? Which one would you most likely be brooding over or talking about with your friends at the end of the day?

Similar to Mr. Sharcke, thoughts or images about things that frighten us are the most distracting, and we tend to focus on them more than we focus on thoughts or images that calm us. Additionally, we tend to pay close attention to and remember threats that we've perceived.[1] This means that we have what we call a threat-detection system, and it has evolved to be always on and to operate in a "better safe than sorry" mode.

Anxiety is one of the most prevalent and challenging forms of human suffering, and it can vary in intensity from mild tension and apprehension to feelings of fear and terror. Anxiety may make us want to run away or scream. It may make us feel heartbroken; it may make us collapse in a protective, tight ball; or it may make us simply go quiet. At times, feelings of pain and shame about anxiety may be so great that we may actually wish to die in order to escape.

During periods of anxiety, our thinking is focused on threats of potential harm and loss, and we can feel an urgent need to run, avoid, freeze, or faint. These responses can be triggered very rapidly and often well before we're aware of it happening. We don't choose to have flushes of anxiety—they're part of our physiological makeup that has evolved over millions of years to protect us from possibly harmful situations. Later, we'll look at this evolutionary history in greater detail, exploring why it is that we might operate with this always-on threat-detection process humming within us. And this book will teach you how to undermine the pervasiveness of the threat-detection system and reclaim your life through compassion and acceptance.

TYPES OF ANXIETY

Every person has a unique, unfolding relationship with his environment. Our distinct personal histories and our moment-to-moment experiences all interact with and influence our emotions, thoughts, and actions. Accordingly, we can notice the differences between us in terms of how anxiety might show up, and also how we might respond to anxious feelings that are unique to and varied in each of us. These variations may relate to what causes us anxiety, how easily our anxiety is triggered, how intense our anxiety is, how frequent it is, the ways we physically and psychologically experience the anxiety, how long the anxiety lasts, and correspondingly how easily or quickly we calm down after becoming anxious.

We also know that anxiety takes many different forms. For example, some people can have intense and sudden physical symptoms, known as panic attacks, that appear to come out of the blue and flush the person with a frightening sense of impending catastrophe. Sometimes the panic is focused on a physical concern, such as fear of having a heart attack. Such symptoms as accelerated heart rate, hyperventilation, and catastrophic predictions about death or going insane are common in people who struggle with panic attacks. Other people, however, can suffer from more generalized anxiety, in which they experience worries throughout the day about a variety of situations. Generalized anxiety can involve hours lost to immersion in negative predictions. Individuals who feel this way may rarely feel safe or fully content.

People with social anxiety can become particularly concerned about social situations, fearing that people might see them as inadequate or inferior and, as a consequence, reject or avoid them. Yet other people focus their attention on the way they feel physically—on their bodily lumps and bumps—constantly worrying about illness and disease. And then there are what we call specific phobias, which are anxieties over specific things, such as spiders, snakes, or heights. While these categories might seem like neat little boxes within which we can classify different sets of problems, in actuality many of us suffer from more than one of these problems.

Anxiety is an important and essential emotion; however, when anxiety causes significant distress or when anxious behavior impairs a person's ability to function—when anxiety negatively affects a person's life—we call this an anxiety disorder.

When we look at statistical evidence, we find that people with anxiety disorders are more likely to experience clinical depression[2] and that high levels of anxiety are associated with a range of health problems, such as cardiovascular difficulties, high blood pressure, diabetes, and chronic fatigue.[3] People who suffer from an anxiety disorder are up to five times more likely to visit their doctor, and they're up to six times more likely to be hospitalized for psychiatric reasons.[4] If, like so many of us, you've lived with high levels of anxiety, just reading these statistics probably makes you feel even more anxious! But this book will help you understand that anxiety doesn't have to lead to such consequences, while at the same time helping you understand how important it is to realize the ways that anxiety can affect our lives.

Think about how high levels of anxiety can affect interpersonal relationships; for example, people might have a fear of abandonment and fear of upsetting others and so, instead of dealing with conflicts by being honest and open, they become submissive, which makes them anxious. The trouble is that the things they're unhappy with don't just go away by themselves, and resentment over feeling submissive, neglected, or disempowered then mixes with anxiety and apprehension, which in turn interferes with the ability to be comfortable in relationships. People with anxiety disorders often experience irritability, are easily distracted, are visibly agitated during social interactions, and focus excessively on themselves. Understandably, these sorts of problems also may affect the quality of their relationships.

HOW COMMON IS ANXIETY?

According to the initial findings of the World Health Organization's global mental health survey,[5] anxiety disorders are the most common psychiatric disorder in all but one of the twenty-six countries included in the survey. Nearly 30 percent of Americans will suffer from an anxiety disorder at some point in their lives, and anxiety disorders represent nearly 33 percent of the entire cost of mental health treatment in the United States.[6] Considerably more people will suffer from problematic anxiety that might not reach the level of a "full disorder."

The vast majority of people with anxiety problems don't come forward for help, partly because they feel ashamed and partly because they feel anxious about the therapeutic process itself: they may be afraid of being prescribed medication; they may fear social stigma; or they may just be afraid of discussing and facing their fears in the presence of someone else. Other people may not be aware of the existence of effective treatment for anxiety.

2

What Is Anxiety, and How Has It Evolved?

Many of my clients are pretty clever—they're quick to ask me why anxiety shows up in the ways that it does and how it is that we seem to be programmed to experience it so intensely at times. "Haven't we evolved beyond need for this emotion?" they ask. "It's not as if a saber-toothed tiger might be creeping up on us. And why do we still have this emotion as a reaction to things known to us, things we know to be nonthreatening?"

When my clients ask whether they might be able to get rid of their anxiety altogether, I often ask them what they think would happen if we could totally, miraculously "zap" their capacity for threat detection out of their minds with some sort of ray. If we did this, what would they be left with as an early warning system of possible threats or dangers? When they thought of it this way, many of my clients realized that, if they didn't have the early warning system, they'd possibly end up being plowed over by a bus or even a bicycle courier as she weaves her way quietly and at high speed through traffic.

For now, though, imagine our ancestors, those early human cave-dwellers, out hunting in the wild. In this situation, a flash of movement in the underbrush might indicate that a vicious predator was about to pounce. This would set our ancestors' hearts racing as they immediately prepared to flee. Those who had a sharp enough threat-detection system would be more likely to survive than those who weren't so anxious or afraid, who might then wind up in the belly of a saber-toothed tiger. Those who survived would pass their threat-detection genes to their children, and so it stands to reason that we wouldn't be here at all if we hadn't emerged from a long line of anxious living beings. But saber-toothed tigers aren't the only threats to be on the lookout for—we may be injured by falling or by getting into fights, or we may become ill by eating or drinking noxious substances. In fact, threats and dangers to our physical and psychological health come in many shapes and sizes, and all of those threats need to be detected and dealt with; however, the human brain has only one basic system for organizing the bodily processes of threat—it's not adaptable to each different type of threat. So, this means that whether you're anxious about meeting new people, anxious about being chased down dark alleys by tigers, anxious about losing your wallet on vacation, or anxious about becoming ill and dying, your basic threat-detection system will stimulate increased anxiety and give you that dreadful bodily sense of anxiety and fear.

BETTER SAFE THAN SORRY...

Our bodies respond to and deal with threats in our environment in a way similar to that of airport security: nothing much gets through to be processed until the threat-detection system has decided it's safe. This system is quick to arouse and slow to relax. As an example, imagine that you're walking home alone at night. You hear a sound behind you—your heart rate jumps, but as you keep walking, you realize that you're not in danger. However, your threat-detection system is still on. It needs an outlet, and so it begins to focus on that lump in your arm that wasn't there yesterday or the possibility that your partner will be in a bad mood when you get home— many different types of small triggers can have big effects on us. The threat-detection system is also similar to a factory default setting, in that its first reaction is to be sensitive to possible threats, in all shapes and sizes.

Once the threat-detection system is activated, certain response systems are set in motion. One well-known system, which you may have heard of, is the "fight, flight, or freeze" system, whereby our bodies and impulses opt for either a quick escape, aggressive action to protect ourselves, or doing neither and freezing on the spot. We don't choose to do any of these—the way our bodies react is instinctive.

Another defensive strategy is to turn to caregivers for comfort and protection if anxiety or fear arises. Our brains have evolved to make us feel calmer and more settled when we're in the presence of people who care for us and whom we think of as protectors. We can see this when we watch how children go to their parents, or their nearest caregivers, for a cuddle when they're upset. Compassion and the kindness of others helps us regulate our hair-trigger threat-response system, which helps regulate our anxiety and in turn helps us function in our day-to-day lives. As we'll see later, children need the care and affection of their caregivers and friends to help them settle down their threat-detection system, as well as teach them how to regulate it themselves and develop their ability to do and confront things that may seem frightening.

Although we might often recognize that our caregivers are crucial to our ability to learn how to cope with anxieties, our friends are also important, particularly as we grow into our teenage years. These people, our caregivers and friends, are called attachment figures. They activate what's called our "soothing response" and shape our ability to regulate anxiety. We learn from them. In our teens, our friends are likely to be the ones we will go with to our first parties; they will encourage us to do healthy things, and sometimes dangerous things, as we face new situations and potentially anxiety-inducing social demands.

Our "affiliation system," which involves our experience of others caring for and about us, is crucial to our ability to respond to anxiety. Compassion-focused therapy (CFT) continually highlights the importance of strengthening the affiliation system from the outside and from within ourselves, and that's why we'll focus on self-compassion-generating exercises later.

I often tell my patients that they were born with an "Always On, Better-Safe-Than-Sorry Problem-Solving Machine" in their minds. Let's follow this idea in more detail to help us understand why we may feel overwhelmed by anxiety.

Just for a moment, imagine that you are a rabbit chomping on some carrots in a vegetable patch somewhere near your warren. Imagine next that, suddenly, you hear a sound in the bushes or see a flash of movement close by. What's the best thing to do? Is this the time to relax and enjoy the cool breeze on your fur? No. This is not the time to chill out, bunny style. Nor should you spend too much time thinking about whether what you sensed is or isn't a threat. This is the time to assume there *is* a threat and to make a break for your rabbithole, as fast as possible. Even if that ominous sound was nothing serious, nine times out of ten, or ninety-nine times out of a hundred, it's still better to run, because that sound could have been alerting you, quite literally, to your impending death. One of my colleagues[1] uses a phrase from evolutionary psychology to describe this scenario, and it has stuck with me as a way to remember the importance of our threat-detection system: "You can skip lunch many times, but you can be lunch only once."

Have you ever watched birds feeding on a lawn? You will see them peck for a few moments, stop, look around, peck again, stop, look around—and very small sounds and movements will startle them and they will fly away, leaving the food behind. You might think *How sad that they don't feel more relaxed and can't just enjoy their meal*; however, as far as we know, the birds aren't feeling sorry for themselves; they are simply working with their always-on threat-detection system and being kept alive with their "better safe than sorry" behavior. Who knows when they'll be pounced on by that tabby from next door?

In some contexts, our brains will take very few risks, because the "hardware" of our brains' "better safe than sorry" threat-detection system is combined with the "software" of our personal and individual history. We know that we often develop unrealistic estimates of how dangerous the world may be; for example, if you ask people the chance of being robbed or physically attacked, they tend to overestimate.

There is an important implication in this: strange as it may seem, our brains are *designed* to make mistakes, in that they are *designed* to regularly overestimate the possibility of threats. Why? Because doing so increases our chances of survival.

We also know that our threat-detection system can take control of the direction and quality of our attention. Imagine that it's the winter holiday season and you're shopping for presents in an outdoor mall. It's crowded and cold, but you're feeling fairly happy, since you're doing something nice for your friends and family. You go to ten shops. In nine shops, people are extremely kind and helpful and you've been able to find exactly the right gifts. You come out of each shop feeling pleased; however, in one of the shops the assistant is very rude and unhelpful. You feel irritated and angry with her and leave feeling annoyed, and without a present. Which shop assistant do think you'll remember at the end of the day? Which one would you talk about with your partner or friends? Chances are your attention will focus on the one person who annoyed you rather than the 90 percent who were kind and helpful. This is normal—our brains are designed by evolution to focus on and remember the things that are negative, threatening, and blocking us. And this is why we need to train our minds to pay attention to the *whole* picture and recognize that sometimes we ignore, or tune out, the positive, helpful things.

Once we become anxious, our minds tend to stay in or return to anxious moments in order to look for confirmation of what we believe to be impending danger. They do this in many ways; for example, your threat-detection system can produce thoughts and images that just pop into your head, even when you are in situations that appear calm. Sometimes these thoughts seem strange to us, and we don't understand why they are showing up. For this reason, they're called intrusive thoughts. Imagine, for a moment, that you had an argument with your boss that was resolved, although it didn't end perfectly. Isn't it likely that such an argument would be replayed over and over again in your mind? Here's another example: After you watch a horror film, you might find disturbing images popping back into your mind even when you don't want them. Those images might make you feel frightened or uneasy, even though you know they're only from a film and not real life. This aspect of being frightened by our memories and by certain images even when we know they are not accurate shows us that our brains can produce stimuli that make us feel anxious even when we know, rationally, that we should feel calm. This is why sometimes simply relying on rationality doesn't work. We will come back to this, but my point now is that one of the key features of a well-functioning human brain is that it will give priority to focusing on threats and thinking about self-protection, even over and above rationality itself.

It is sometimes said that cognitive therapy (from which CFT borrows many techniques) is all about looking at the evidence for and against our negative thoughts, and finding out the truth of our thinking; however, it may not always be helpful or convenient to test the truth of our thinking. It may be more useful or easier to base our behavior on what works, moment by moment. After all, if you have to escape from the sixth floor of a burning apartment building via the fire escape, it's probably not the most helpful strategy to look down and focus on the fact that if you fall, you'll die.[2] Instead, you should focus on what can help you climb down or get away so that you are most likely to survive. So even when your threat-detection system is giving you perfectly accurate information (if you fall, you'll die), it's not always the most helpful or compassionate thing to focus on.

EVOLUTION AND FORMS OF ANXIETY

Many fears and anxieties are learned in some way, whether they're widely shared or highly individual. There are some fears that evolution has made sure we can acquire very easily, such as fear of snakes and fear of spiders, even though the fact is that most of you reading this are far more likely to be killed or injured by electricity or by slipping on a wet floor than by a snake or a spider. However, electricity and wet floors haven't been around for very long (compared to snakes and spiders) and haven't affected our evolution; thus, we need a lot of personal experience to develop a fear of them. A fear of snakes or spiders is a common anxiety based on the experiences of our ancestors.

Examples of How Our Current Fears Relate to Threats That Our Evolutionary Ancestors Faced[3]

Current Fear	Threats Throughout Evolution
Fear of snakes/spiders	Difficult to detect and potentially dangerous in our natural ancestral environment
Agoraphobia	Dangerous environment and too distant from a safe base
Claustrophobia	Being trapped in confined spaces and places
Social anxiety	Social put-down and rejection
Paranoia	Group attack or rejection, abandonment from group protection
Hypochondria	Threat to physical health
Compulsive disorder	Potential contaminants/illness/disease and also avoidance of spreading disease
Obsessive disorder	Having made errors or done harm
General anxiety	Dangerous environments

One of the reasons we like going to the cinema or watching films at home is that the story lines allow us to see and identify with other people who have anxieties and fears and who are facing dangers and hopefully coping with them; however, we can also acquire phobias in this way, through observation. The psychologists and anxiety experts Michael Cook and Susan Mineka[4] ran a series of experiments in the 1980s that showed to one group of monkeys another group of monkeys who were frightened of a toy snake when it was presented to them. The observing group learned to become similarly frightened when toy snakes were introduced to their cage. The observing group were also shown another group of monkeys that were reacting fearfully to a flower; however, the observing group showed no fear when the flower was introduced to their own cage. It was thought that perhaps they may have had experiences with other plants and could recognize a flower as harmless. Whatever the exact mechanisms involved were, these experiments showed that monkeys' evolutionary history with snakes had likely primed them—and other primates like them, such as us humans—to be more likely to acquire a fear of snakes, even by observation of others acting fearfully, than they might learn to fear something harmless, such as a flower.

This is particularly significant in the context of concerns about TV and other media that increasingly focus on violence or on shaming and rejecting people in competitions that throw out a contestant each week, for example. It's unclear what the impact of such programs is, apart from telling us that we are constantly being judged and can easily be found wanting. This is unfortunate, given that the fear of social rejection is a major source of anxiety for humans because our survival has depended on acceptance and sharing, and given also that our fears are often shaped and easily developed by our current social environment.

Remember Jennifer and her first panic attack, on the subway? Well, entrapment is a natural danger to humans, and if we are in a state of anxiety, tired, or stressed, our brains tend to flick through our files of potential dangers, spot one that seems to fit, and then set off the alarm. This sounds like what may have happened with Jennifer, who was already in an anxious state: her brain likened the experience of being in a closed subway car to being trapped and, as a result, pushed the alarm button. This is why she found relief when she went out into the fresh air. In fact, it's common for people to become claustrophobic if they're already slightly anxious. In some ways what's more extraordinary is the fact that people by the millions go to work on trains and subways, often crushed together!

But just as we can learn that something is dangerous, we can also learn that something that triggers our threat-detection system is safe. This is fundamental to our understanding of how we can regulate our senses and regulate our threat-response system: if you've experienced a high degree of anxiety in a certain situation, it's likely that being in that situation again, or even being in a *similar* situation, will trigger your threat response. If when I was a child I suffered an embarrassing failure in delivering a speech about ancient history, I still may quiver a bit when I have to stand before a group of colleagues and speak about sales figures, for example.

To really understand how we learn our patterns of response to anxiety, we need to look at how we and other animals learn from our interactions with our environments.

Anxiety Learned by Association

So far, a great deal of what we've discussed has been about the way we have evolved to be able to react to and deal with threats in our environment; however, we have also evolved to easily acquire feelings of anxiety and physical and mental responses to those feelings.

Behavioral scientists often describe two basic learning processes that contribute to the way we learn to respond to situations. The first is often called classical conditioning and was discovered by the Russian physiologist Ivan Pavlov (1849–1936), who became interested in how our stomachs respond to food or to the promise of food. It was well known that the smell of food could make dogs salivate; what Pavlov discovered was that if he regularly sounded a bell before giving the dogs their dinner, the dogs would begin to salivate at the sound, regardless of whether food was produced afterward. Normally, the ringing bell would not make an animal salivate, but these dogs had *acquired* that physical response (salivating) because of an *association* (the sound of the bell signaling that food would be dished out).

"Classical conditioning," or learning by association, has become important to our understanding of anxiety because we have found that our threat-response system responds not only to perceived threats, but also to things we associate with perceived threats. This is called generalization, or discrimination learning. Suppose that every time a bell was rung, Pavlov's dogs were given a mild electric shock instead of food. Rather than a tail-wagging, salivating, "where's my food?" response, the dogs would then develop a cowering fear response to the bell. This fearful response to the ringing of the bell is known as "aversive" conditioning, but it is still learning by association. And from this we can see that the bell can acquire any kind of physiological effect depending on what it's paired, or associated, with, and this means that almost any neutral stimulus, such as a bell, can create physiological reactions in us because of what we've linked it with, or what it has been linked to, previously. Likewise, if something has caused you anxiety in the past, you will associate this certain something—be it a hairy spider, giving a speech, or a crowded train—with threat in the future. Your brain and threat-response system have learned to react to it with anxiety.

Here's a different scenario: Imagine that you're a child sleeping lightly in your bed, when suddenly you're awakened by the smashing of a window in another room. Sensing the hurried, purposeful, rumbling movement of a team of burglars, you automatically feel fear and a desire to get to safety. In such a situation you might learn to associate some of the other elements of the environment, such as the time of night, the furniture in the room, or the ticking of the clock, with this moment of danger and terror. Later in life, your fear from that situation might generalize into anxiety when you go to bed or into a startled response to noises outside of your bedroom. As a result, you might fear going back to bed; thus, as a result of this burglary you learn, or are "conditioned," to fear your bedroom because what you felt when you were there (fear) is something you associate with the burglary. An otherwise neutral element of the environment (your bedroom) has become associated with a frightening event (a burglary).

Okay. So now you know that anxiety can be triggered because of what you've learned in the past. But you should also understand that anxiety can be triggered without any learning at all, which includes our responses to such things as sudden loud noises; aggressive, threatening people; large open spaces; animals coming toward us; and heights—our basic anxiety responses can be associated with all kinds of things. Let's look at another example. Imagine a child—let's call him Fred—whose father was aggressive and who, if Fred had made him angry, would send him to his room to wait; then, eventually, Fred's dad would enter the room, scream at him, and beat him. Understandably, Fred was very anxious when he waited in his room for his father to deliver the abuse. When Fred grew up, one day he went to see a new doctor for a checkup. He walked into the examination room and immediately began to feel overwhelming anxiety. Not knowing exactly what was happening or why, he was very alarmed and disoriented; however, after a few moments, it dawned on him that the wallpaper in the exam room was similar to the wallpaper in his boyhood room. Through associative learning and classical conditioning, Fred had unconsciously remembered how he felt when he was a child, and this memory helped to recreate his physical and mental feelings of anxiety.

This "body memory," as we now call it, can be somewhat controversial because it is sometimes used to support theories about repressed memories. In CFT we aren't really concerned with these, and when we use the term "body memory," we simply mean the way that our nervous system, via our physical body and our mental functioning—our brains—can involuntarily invoke a response that we have learned and which we then physically feel. It can be triggered by any of the senses: sight, hearing, taste, smell, or touch.

Here's another example. Imagine you're at a party. You enjoy a beer or a piece of cake, but within a little while you feel quite ill, and soon you're vomiting violently. Eventually you recover, and after a few weeks you've forgotten about it at the conscious level. You go to another party, but as you step through the door somebody gives you a beer or a piece of cake. What do you think happens to your body? Just the smell of the beer or the sight of the cake could give you a flash of nausea; your body remembers immediately. Because you "forgot" the previous incident, you might not be able to fully understand your reaction to something seemingly harmless.

A part of the brain called the amygdala is responsible for body memory. The amygdala is active from birth, whereas the hippocampus, the part of the brain that allows us to remember time and place—to remember when and where bad things happen to us—matures and becomes active much later. Some researchers think that we can acquire body-memory anxieties before we can accurately locate them in time and place and that this could be a reason some people experience certain types of anxiety that they can't identify the cause of, or any specific reason for. In CFT we aim to develop a healthy response to our anxiety through new emotional experiences that directly influence and affect how the amygdala works.

There is one other aspect to anxiety and conditioning that affects us, and this is the fact that we can become affected by, and respond to, not only external events—things in the world around us—but also internal events, things inside our minds. Many years ago, a behavioral psychologist[5] noted that if children are constantly punished for being angry, they will become anxious about being punished; over time their feelings of anger will become associated with the expectation of punishment, and the expectation of punishment activates anxiety. After a while, the system or cycle short-circuits;

thus, the feelings of anger automatically trigger feelings of anxiety. What happens then is that when conflicts arise, instead of feeling anger and learning to be assertive, the person simply becomes overwhelmed with anxiety about her own potential anger. There are many therapies that suggest that sometimes anxiety is driven by a person's inability to deal with other emotions, including anger. So if you suffer from anxiety, it's always worth thinking about how you deal with conflicts and how comfortable you are with your anger.

There are other internal events that can become associated with anxiety. For example, sexual fantasies and sexual feelings are common sources of anxiety. If you are homosexual but live in a place that is extremely hostile toward homosexuality, you may become anxious about your feelings and desires. As soon as they pop into your mind, you might begin to have an anxiety attack. Or, if you live somewhere that is extremely conservative, you may experience anxiety about your liberal sexual views and beliefs, which seem to be in contrast to the status quo.

We'll come back to the fear of such internal events later. For now, it's important to note the fact that sometimes we can have automatically anxious responses without realizing the reasons or emotions behind them.

Anxiety Learned by Consequences

So the first type of learning we've explored is called classical conditioning, or learning by association, and it relates to the way our brains and bodies automatically respond to certain triggers and how some new things in our environment can become associated with these triggers and evoke a response similar to the one we experienced originally.

The second type of learning is based on consequences. In this type of learning, whether we're likely to repeat a behavior depends on whether what happens as a result (or as a perceived result) of our behavior feels like reward or punishment. (The technical term for this type of learning is "operant conditioning.")

Put plainly, if we repeatedly experience a pleasant or desirable consequence after we behave in a certain way, we're more likely to repeat that behavior. If we experience an unpleasant or painful consequence after behaving in a certain way, we're less likely to behave that way again. For example, if a child returns home after her curfew and is punished by not being allowed to play any video games for a weekend, this punishment may reduce this curfew-breaking behavior in the future. Conversely, if a child completes her homework on time and is then praised by her parents and they give her a bonus in her weekly allowance, this reward might contribute to more frequent timely homework-completion behavior. Now, we all know that learning, and particularly parenting, isn't quite that simple, but these are the basic principles that allow people to learn to behave in a certain way after repeated experiences of reward or punishment for that behavior.

When it comes to the dynamics of learning, anxiety can seem very tricky. Both of the learning processes we've looked at contribute to our tendency to re-experience anxiety over the course of our lives. If we look at the example of a fear of social situations, we can begin to see how learning theory (the scientific theory about learning) might shed a little more light on how anxiety operates. More importantly, we can get a sense of how our best efforts to avoid anxiety can actually make it worse.

Imagine that Jennifer, whom we met earlier, was bookish, reserved, yet friendly when she was a teenager. Imagine that perhaps one day she went to a high school dance and was filled with hopes to be popular, make friends, or just feel approved of by a group of her peers. She wore her best outfit and tried to be "cool." At the dance, some other teenage girls, who were hungry to assert their own place at the top of the high school popularity food chain, decided to bully and tease her. They joked about her being a "geek" and laughed at her as she danced. Because of this experience, Jennifer later began to associate social events with being mocked. This example of classical conditioning trained her to feel fear, experience self-doubt, and expect to be bullied when she approaches social situations.

How might Jennifer respond to invitations to social events and gatherings in the future? Well, you've seen that we've evolved with an always-on, "better safe than sorry" threat-detection system that helps us to steer clear of danger. And in this case Jennifer's threat-detection system responds by avoiding social situations that provoke anxiety. With this avoidance, we can see the beginning of learning by consequences, which builds on the foundation of classical conditioning, or learning by association. And these together help establish and then maintain Jennifer's anxiety.

By avoiding a social event, Jennifer relieves her anxiety and releases any tension in the immediate or short term. That release actually rewards and then reinforces her behavior, which she'll then repeat. And the cycle continues. In this case, her behavior is worrying about, and becoming anxious about, going to a party. Paradoxically, her avoidance is actually training her to feel more anxiety in the long term: by avoiding social experiences, Jennifer is consistently teaching herself to remain afraid of contact with other people; however, this isn't the end of the story, because one of the key points of CFT is that it often depends on the degree of helpfulness and kindness we have around us when we experience these kinds of events. We know, for example, that anxious parents tend to increase their children's anxiety, because if their children have been bullied, for example, the parents will encourage their children to avoid subsequent social situations in which they may be bullied again. This action makes sense to them: Why would they want to see their children so unhappy? Why would they encourage them back into those situations that are obviously unpleasant? Yet there are many good reasons for doing so: to teach the child to confront the bullies or any other difficult situation, how to deal with the situation better than by avoiding it altogether, to be assertive, how to find other friends, and how to cope with unpleasant feelings. We learn nothing from avoidance other than avoidance, which may reinforce the experience of anxiety itself and may make us critical of ourselves for our behavior and then feel unhappy about missing out, which is typical of children who feel bullied. Some people even begin to dislike themselves for the thing they're bullied about, whether it be shyness or being overweight or being a bit clumsy. So how is that child going to overcome or learn to work on her anxiety when she is also self-critical?

But if you were Jennifer's friends, or her parents who weren't anxious, what would you do? Would you encourage her to avoid a similar situation? Would you be critical and force her to go out? Or would you be understanding and compassionate, but also encouraging and supportive, step by step, to help develop her confidence? The chances are that you'd do the latter, and that's key to understanding the steps in CFT. You see? You already have the inner wisdom of how to deal with your anxiety, because when you think about an example like this you probably know exactly what to do; however, when it comes to your own anxiety you may well have critical thoughts about it, try to avoid or suppress it, or feel ashamed of it, rather than feel kind, supportive, encouraging, and understanding toward yourself, as you would toward Jennifer.

So, even though we have intuitive wisdom to be compassionate, we can still fall back into a spiral of anxiety and avoidance, which is sometimes called safety behavior and which can lead to an amplification of our response to anxiety and to an increase in our suffering. It seems that the more we try to avoid, change, or suppress our experiences of anxiety, the more the anxiety is intensified in the long term. Psychological research has revealed that our best attempts to stifle or push away thoughts and feelings often backfire.[6]

In a classic example, imagine that you agree to take part in a psychology experiment at a university. The experimenters give you a simple set of instructions: "For the next five minutes, don't think of a purple gorilla. Every time you think of a purple gorilla, make a check mark on this piece of paper in front of you." How many check marks might you make? Most people will make a heck of a lot. When we try not to think of that gorilla, there it is again, purple as ever. The reason suppression operates like this is straightforward—you have to keep checking that you're suppressing your thoughts, and in order to do this you have to keep revisiting what you're trying to suppress just to make sure nothing creeps out around the edges. And because you've associated *not* suppressing with something that is frightening, your fear system will keep pushing you to remember it.

Beyond what you've learned so far, it's important to recognize that every time you think, *Don't think of a purple gorilla*, you've just thought of a purple gorilla. Similarly, if you're telling yourself not to think certain anxiety-provoking thoughts, you're thinking those anxiety-provoking thoughts.

However, what happens if we turn the experiment on its head? In our contrasting experiment the instructions are simply as follows: "Observe whatever thoughts you might have, and feel free to think anything at all. If you happen to think about a purple gorilla, please make a check mark on this piece of paper." Given the meandering nature of mental activity, your thoughts would likely wander through all sorts of topics. From time to time that purple gorilla might pop up in your imagination. It is, after all, a rather odd image to consider. We can reliably predict, though, that you won't be making as many check marks when you allow your mind free rein. That gorilla won't show up as often if you aren't actively wrapped up in trying to push its image away.

Part of your training in developing self-compassion and mindful awareness will involve changing your relationship to your experiences, and this is not done by struggling with and avoiding such emotions as anxiety. Self-compassion and loving-kindness allow us to develop an openness to our present-moment experiences and to then remain connected to difficult feelings and to develop new ways of responding to those things that scare us. In this way, we can witness our own pain and fear and develop the ability to respond with kindness, patience, and effective action.

Traditional behavior therapy trains people to remain in the presence of those things that trigger anxiety until the anxiety response has run its course. For example, if I were afraid of heights, my behavioral therapist might take me, one step at a time, to a window on a very high floor of a tall building. I'd edge closer to the window, staying with each step until the anxiety decreased, and then I'd take another step, slowly teaching my body that everything was actually okay. Because I wouldn't act on my fears, my threat-response system would gradually settle down. The lesson would be anxiety-provoking at first, but if I remained in the presence of what I feared, or what triggered my fear, without avoiding it, my anxiety would likely gradually decrease. In time, with repeated learning experiences, I'd be able to respond differently and without fear or avoidance. This type of therapy is often referred to as exposure, and it has been proven to be effective for treating problems with anxiety.

EXPOSURE WITH COMPASSION

While exposure has a good track record in the treatment of anxiety, CFT goes beyond this method; it seeks to do more than just train people to exhaust their anxiety responses. Imagine that you're in therapy to deal with the anxiety caused by your fear of heights. Imagine on the one hand that your therapist seems competent, very understanding, patient, and caring; she smiles at you and encourages you. You feel safe with her. On the other hand, imagine that your therapist seems competent but is also standoffish and doesn't smile very much; she tells you what to do but doesn't particularly encourage you or seem friendly toward you. Which therapist do you want, and which do you think you can have the most success with? Not a difficult question, is it? Likewise, we are more able to engage with things that frighten us if we are in a supportive environment. Children in particular can engage with things that are frightening if people whom they trust are around them to encourage them and give them friendly signals. You can see examples of this for yourself: search for "Visual Cliff Experiment" on YouTube.

CFT points out that just as the experience of understanding, kindness, encouragement, and genuine feelings of being cared about will help us engage in things that are difficult, so too will developing this attitude and emotional tone toward ourselves be immensely helpful. When they first come to see me, many of my clients lack this inner compassionate tone toward themselves and, if anything, dislike themselves for being anxious, which they often think of as a weakness or an inadequacy. At the very least, they're hostile toward their anxiety. As we'll see, training ourselves to be self-compassionate activates an innate emotion-regulation system, which involves a deep appreciation of suffering and a loving aspiration to alleviate that suffering. It stems from the same evolutionary source as a mother's care and attention toward her young. When we have self-compassion we can remain in the presence of difficult feelings with a wide, accepting, flexible awareness, and as a result we can learn new, workable, and engaging ways of responding to even the most challenging and anxiety-provoking situations, thoughts, and sensations.

3

Anxiety, Compassion, and Our Ongoing Interactions with the World

We can see how millions of years of evolution coupled with our unique personal histories can make us particularly sensitized to anxious feelings and that this can lead to trouble. But have no doubt that anxiety can be a lifesaver, too. Our awareness of danger can keep our physical bodies safe, and it can also help us in other ways by alerting us to all sorts of things that we need to pay attention to in our personal, professional, and academic lives. For example, if we become anxious before an exam, we may make some special efforts to ensure we prepare as best we can. Similarly, feeling a little bit extra aware of danger on the highway might mean that we pay closer attention to our driving. You might be anxious if you feared your child was ill, and this might make you call the doctor just that much sooner. Anxiety is basically a system designed by evolution to help us and to guide us toward actions that may protect us. So far so good, except that it doesn't always work quite so smoothly, and when it doesn't it can be a real hassle and cause all sorts of distress.

Enduring a hair-trigger threat-detection system is like having smoke detectors that keep going off when you use the stove. When our anxiety thresholds are chronically raised, which can happen when we live in a stressful environment, our anxiety can become an unwelcome guest. It's still part of our basic protection system, but now it's showing up when we don't need it to, feeling too intense, and lasting too long.

In order to understand our anxiety response and eventually reach a place of safety and calm, even when our fears are triggered, it will help to recognize that anxiety emerges through some important interactions between us and our environment. Our personal history can contribute to how and why we feel anxious, just as our genetic history has contributed to our capacity for threat detection. The particular stressful situations that we face in our everyday lives are also factors that can lead to our anxiety levels feeling problematic. Our moods, our relationships, and many other aspects of our lives can help trigger our threat-detection system in ways that don't really help us and that contribute to our suffering.

When I think of my client Jennifer, whom we met in the first chapter, I remember the many elements that came together for her that day on the subway to create a perfect storm that led to her panic attack. Let's look at a few of these factors to help us understand just how anxiety problems can manifest themselves.

The day that she first called me, Jennifer was facing a great deal of stress in the form of strict new evaluation programs that had been put in place in her school system that year. Her new term was about to begin, and she desperately wanted to live up to the relentlessly high standards of the administration. The engine of her mind kept churning away about this, seeking new ways to ensure that she'd be perceived as above average or even superior.

On top of this, a few weeks earlier, her boyfriend of many years had told her that he needed to take a break from their relationship and explained that he'd prefer to date other people, for a while at least. This was very sad for her, because she was really devoted to him and had envisioned they'd marry and live happily ever after. She hadn't, however, allowed herself to tell him about this vision.

Beyond this, Jennifer had been raised by parents who were completely wrapped up in the idea of success and achievement and who focused much of their effort on pushing her to be in complete control of her emotions. They were involved, supportive, and caring parents in principle, but their beliefs about emotional control and achievement eclipsed their ability to nurture, accept, and soothe their children. In Jennifer's family, effectiveness, conscientiousness, and academic excellence were prized above emotional expression, uncertainty, and spontaneity. Any hint that she was feeling out of control led Jennifer to suspect that there was something fundamentally damaged, flawed, and unlovable about her. In turn, she relied on avoidance-based coping strategies, such as avoiding social contact, restricting her expressions of emotion, and attempting to suppress thoughts and emotions, all of which trained her to feel more and more anxiety in a range of different situations.

Much later in her therapy, Jennifer tearfully admitted that she always suspected that she'd eventually lose her mind and die alone in a psychiatric hospital. She believed this because she'd been taught that her emotions amounted to weakness and, if uncontrolled, would lead to insanity. No one had explained to her, or understood themselves, that anxiety is a natural part of life or that anxious feelings would rise and fall like waves, as do all mental experiences. As Jennifer and I worked together, we gradually discovered the way these different threads of her life had interwoven and created a response system that was entirely preoccupied with threat detection. As a result, anxiety and a very real terror around the basic act of living were virtually destined to dominate her experiences: she constantly felt fearful and ashamed. We can see, though, that Jennifer's anxiety and her way of trying to deal with it weren't her fault.

If we stand back and recognize that our brains are built to generate powerful emotions, we can also realize that our experience of these emotions is absolutely not our fault. Moreover, if early in life we don't learn what our emotions and internal responses mean, or learn healthy and functional ways to deal with them, our inner lives can become particularly problematic. Again, it's important to know that this is no fault of our own.

Perhaps now would be a good time to take a minute—maybe close your eyes—to focus on the fact that your anxiety is not your fault. Slowly, kindly, and gently say over and over again to yourself, either out loud or in your mind, *It's not my fault*. Note any resistance—any other voice that says, *Yes, but....* This step and this recognition will help you begin your journey to self-compassion, into letting go of shame and blame.

Understand that your mind has been constructed to feel anxiety and that certain events or experiences in your life have in some way activated the system in you. If you begin to develop a noncritical, kind, and understanding voice, you are taking the first step toward a compassionate approach to your anxiety. Don't worry if this seems more difficult than it sounds; it's common for people to struggle with being kind to themselves and to stop blaming themselves for their anxiety.

You didn't choose to have a brain that is capable of intense anxiety, nor did you choose to have anxiety difficulties; they really are not your fault. However, you can learn to be honest about them, change your relationship with them, and live with them in conditions of greater ease.

ANXIETY, COMPASSION, AND YOUR TWO BRAINS

We can use the idea of having two brains to understand that, in fact, we have a number of "different brains" that we can look at from the top to the bottom or from left to right or even back to front, because different areas of the brain are responsible for different functions of our behavior. We like to think that the functions of the brain always work as a team—and often they do—but sometimes different functions within the brain can conflict with one another. What I want to bring to your attention is the fact that our brains are formed so that they're roughly divided into two regions that represent different stages of evolution.

Of course, this is an oversimplification; a neuroscientist, or even a ten-year-old with access to a computer can show you full-color, three-dimensional representations of a whole host of different brain regions, each one involved in different parts of the way we function; however, it's useful to notice two distinct aspects of the brain: the "old brain" and the "new brain." For many years neuroscientists have been pointing to the importance of distinguishing between motivation systems and emotional systems on the one hand and the more recently evolved systems that enable us to think and have a sense of self on the other.

A simple way of thinking about this is that there are parts of the human brain that we can trace back hundreds of millions of years and other parts that developed much more recently. Some scientists talk about how the oldest parts of the brain are involved with the four "F"s: feeding, fighting, fleeing, and…having sex; because we're mammals, our "old brain" has also developed in ways to make us able to care for infants. This "old brain" is also concerned with basic emotions, such as anxiety, anger, and joy; sexual interest and motives; forming friendships; and belonging to groups. Our "new brain," which is distinctively human, gives us the capacity for conscious thought, reasoning, imagining the future, and so on.

CFT uses this understanding of the different parts of the brain, albeit in a simplified way, to help us make sense of the complicated link between thinking and the systems in our bodies that produce often very strong physical and impulsive urges. And, again, these are our "factory default settings." Indeed, one of the important aspects of CFT is the consideration of how old and new brain systems interact. Obviously, humans have a uniquely large capacity for language, imagination, planning, and conceptualization—not even our most complex and intelligent animal relatives share this capacity. We can imagine the future and worry about it; remember and fret about the past; and wonder about how we're thought of by others. We can develop sophisticated verbal theories about who in our office likes us, who has it in for us, and what their specific reasons for their opinions might be. All of this winds up expanding the number of things we can feel anxious about and increases the likelihood of holding anxiety in our minds.

Animals' mental activity is very different; for example, no matter how clever they may be, monkeys don't take their pulse, and they don't look at their reflections and worry about putting on too much weight or going bald. Zebras don't stay up at night worrying about where the lions will be in the morning, and they certainly don't worry about their children's careers.

The distinctive nature of human experience has to do with our fantastically evolved, blindingly efficient "new brain"; however, the structures this rests on and interacts with are parts of our brains that are older, in evolutionary terms. And in order to understand anxiety, compassion, and our emotional lives, it helps to understand this "old brain" and how it functions.

The philosopher Alan Watts once emphasized, "We don't come into the world, we come out of it." The entire spectrum of our motivations, emotions, aspirations, and mental capacities has emerged from a complex, ongoing process of evolution, which allows us to trace the genetic and historical roots of our inner and outer behaviors. The brain systems involved with some of our most basic emotions, such as anger, fear, and disgust, are millions of years older than our species[1] and, as we touched on earlier, animals have been functioning in "fight, flight, or freeze" mode to survive and protect themselves for a very long time. Our brain structures and nervous-system interactions that support these protection emotions and behaviors are similar to those in less-evolved mammals and even in reptiles. These structures and interactions are what we're referring to when we speak about the "old brain."

Studies of chimpanzees engaged in the pursuit of sexual and social relationships show that they strive for dominance and status in their own social hierarchies and that they're capable of looking after one another. They communicate with each other and ask for help or protection in times of danger and need. Chimpanzees team up to hunt, and when they're frightened they seek comfort in one another's company. Apart from chimps, such animals as the common crow, which happens to be a very clever bird, can roughly deduce the intentions of other animals in their environment. Crows call to one another to warn of danger and either compete for or share their resources.[2] A great many of the emotions, motives, and social behaviors that we think of as fundamentally human have actually been present in other species for far longer than we have been renting space on this planet. Some of the most prominent features of old-brain emotions are anger, anxiety, sadness, joy, and lust; old-brain behaviors include responses of fight, flight, withdrawal, or direct engagement with another organism or situation. In the realm of relationships, we can see such features as the pursuit of sex, power, and status; tribalism; and attachment behaviors toward others.

In addition to these capacities we share with other animals, we humans have a wide range of capacities related to our "new brain." A lot of these new-brain capacities have to do with language, thinking, imagination, planning, and problem solving.

Our "new brain" makes us uniquely capable of crafting symbolic mental and verbal representations of our environment and ourselves. We can understand the world around us by making a simple observation, such as "That rock looks bigger than that other rock," or by more complex means, such as theoretical calculus or the poetic wordplay of Shakespeare. One of the miracles of new-brain capacity is that we can learn through conditioning and through the consequences of our actions, but also through observation, deduction, and indirect experience. We also have an amazing ability to be self-aware, which allows us to observe even our own acts of observation.

Overall, the "new brain" gives us the ability to imagine, plan, think, and communicate by using written and spoken language and also to construe our sense of self and our self-awareness.

How does this relate to anxiety? Well, part of the problem with anxiety involves the collision of old-brain emotions and purposes with the fascinating capacities of our "new brain." Let's return to the example of Jennifer to look at how her two brains may have been interacting when she struggled with anxiety.

Jennifer's "old brain" had set her up to respond to any perceived threat with a rapid "fight, flight, or freeze" response, based on the "better safe than sorry" principle. Her "old brain" was programmed to seek status, approval of the group, and attachment to others and to fear being shunned in social interactions and getting trapped in potentially dangerous environments. As we saw, her personal history emphasized and reinforced the act of seeking acceptance and the expectation of rejection in social situations, and as a result she was conditioned to have an anxiety response in a situation that might involve social evaluation. We also saw the threat to her romantic attachment, and such a threat can also raise our anxiety threshold, as it did for her. It's common for people who've experienced a separation or a major loss to experience increased anxiety, and this is another example of the interaction between anxiety and our sense of safety created through our secure and compassionate relationships. All of this—the motivations, the learned behavior, and the emotions—can be thought of as originating in the "old brain."

But it doesn't stop there. Jennifer was bright, and she had lots of finely honed new-brain capacities, such as self-awareness. While she lay awake at night, the stirrings of her "old brain" interacted with her "new brain" and took the form of a stream of worrisome predictions about how the rest of her life would unfold. If we remind ourselves of Jennifer's early history and some of the events that had recently occurred in her life, we can notice how she'd become much more inwardly self-focused. She'd tell herself: *I'm going to be like this forever—I know it. Everyone at school can see I'm a nervous wreck, and there's just no way out. I'm a fraud. I try to seem so competent, but I'm barely functioning. Who'd want to be with a person like this? No wonder my boyfriend left me. I'm going to die alone after living in a squalid apartment with thirty cats!* And while she thought about this, her "new brain" was unspooling corresponding images. She'd see herself being scowled at and could almost smell the dank apartment where she imagined she'd grow old, all alone. Her "new brain" had a necessary tendency to respond to imaginary things as if they were real, and this meant that her heart would pound, her stomach would churn, and her body and mind would prepare themselves for what they perceived to be a life-threatening situation, despite the fact that she was lying safely in bed, miles away from such an experience. But her "old brain" tended to narrow and focus her attention to help her avoid potential danger, whether real or imagined. And when she then tried to suppress potentially distressing thoughts and feelings, her efforts backfired and instead kept her focused on her recurring anxieties. From this scenario, we can see how anxiety can be stirred up when old-brain activity mingles with our new-brain abilities.

4

Toward the Compassionate Mind: An Evolution in Our Understanding of Anxiety through Mindfulness, Acceptance, and Compassion

Talk therapy and psychiatric medication are relatively recent developments that took shape during the last century; however, people have been devising clever ways of coping with anxiety and other difficult emotions since the earliest days of civilization.

As early as 3400 BC, people used opiates to alter their consciousness and to communicate with the gods during rituals.[1] Throughout history and in cultures the world over, shamans, mystics, and tribal leaders have been consulted when people faced emotional problems or needed guidance. Some consultations occurred in face-to-face meetings or rituals, in which herbs might have been prescribed as medicine. There's evidence that yoga and meditations to calm and center the mind in response to anxiety and other troubling emotions were in use in India more than 3,000 years ago.[2]

In his seminal work *The Observing Self*, Arthur Deikman traces the tradition of psychotherapy back through what he sees as its historical roots[3] and suggests that the work modern psychotherapists engage in descends from centuries of meetings between priests or mystics and people who felt troubled and wanted to talk about their problems. Centuries ago, efforts to work through difficult emotions and problems may have had a spiritual rationale, but as our scientific understanding of the brain, the mind, and behavior has evolved, so have our theories about anxiety and our methods for treatment.

Since the advent of modern psychotherapy (over the past 120 years or so), different ideas about the causes of anxiety have emerged. Each new idea brought about new suggestions for how to deal with the problem. Although much of their work is based on the science of learning, behaviorists—such as Ivan Pavlov, whom we mentioned earlier—have also suggested that some of our fears are inherited and due to our biological makeup. Others, such as Pavlov's contemporary, the groundbreaking psychotherapist Sigmund Freud, believed that our behavior is the result of the suppressed wishes and desires that we harbor in our subconscious. Years later, in the late 1960s and early 1970s, rapidly advancing computer technology and advances in research about cognition and perception led to what's now known as the Cognitive Revolution in psychology: rather than focusing on supposedly subconscious desires, or looking at models of animal behavior, psychotherapists became increasingly interested in how humans process information. Based on the work of Aaron T. Beck and Albert Ellis, schools of "cognitive therapy" emerged[4] and promoted the idea that it's often our interpretations of reality, patterns of thinking, and negative biases that lead to problems with anxiety.

According to a cognitive therapist, if someone has a rush of anxiety and experiences a racing heart, this is not a problem in itself, but if thoughts of losing control or having a heart attack then come up, the person may panic. The process that takes the anxiety to a problematic level, according to cognitive therapists, is the negative automatic thoughts that we have about perceived threats. We know that many people naturally feel somewhat anxious when meeting new people or socializing (this is why alcohol is so commonly consumed at parties), and of course some people are shyer than others. Cognitive theory suggests that social anxiety becomes problematic when people start to buy into the perception that others see them as inferior, inadequate, boring, or stupid (for example). Many of us also have various anxieties about our physical health—after all, none of us wants to become ill, be incapacitated, or die. However, few of us suffer from such health-related anxiety; rather, for most of us, worries about health come and go without our being overly focused on them. But people with hypochondriacal anxieties have frequent, intense thoughts that they could be ill, even if their physician has just given them a clean bill of health. They may think *Maybe the doctor missed something, or maybe something has changed between the time I visited the doctor and now.* This leads them to seek repeated reassurances, each of which serves to placate their worry for only a while.

Another side effect of anxiety is vivid imagination; for example, people who have problems with panic can have clear visions or mental images of themselves keeling over and collapsing; people who have social anxiety might have images of other people ridiculing them or secretly wanting to distance themselves from them.

The cognitive-therapy approach focuses on the meanings that we give to different triggers and experiences and seeks to help people overcome anxiety by noticing anxiety-stimulating thoughts and directly changing such thinking in order to reduce distress. This can happen through a systematic questioning of negative automatic thoughts, done in therapy sessions and in homework exercises.

All these approaches have some merit; however, good science always moves on in an effort to improve understanding and the effectiveness of interventions. Over the past decade, a quiet revolution has taken place in the sciences of the mind and psychotherapy. Eastern mind-training traditions and Western psychology have come together in an unprecedented fashion, allowing the development of new psychotherapies that build on and add to our understanding of anxiety and how to cope with it. Such concepts as mindfulness, acceptance, compassion, and self-compassion that were once solely associated with Eastern meditative practices or dismissed by psychologists as "new age" are now central therapeutic concepts and the subject of worldwide research.

Many of these approaches focus on anxiety's ability to easily grab our attention and hold it firmly in its grasp. Mindfulness and acceptance-based psychotherapies point out that, with patience and awareness, we can choose what we pay attention to, or attend to, moment by moment. We can also learn to pay attention to aspects of our minds that are specifically designed to regulate and calm down our threat-detection systems: just as a child anxiously runs back to mother for a calming, loving embrace, so too can we direct our attention to inner images that evoke feelings of kindness, understanding, and support for a calming and soothing effect.

The first major applications of Buddhist-influenced psychotherapy were based on various forms of meditation, a term that may sound a bit religious but is really a sort of catchall for a variety of methods used to train our minds. These methods share a common theme, which involves the training of a greater, nonjudgmental, accepting experience of our inner life. Meditation is simply a way of slowing down and paying attention to what's going on in our minds, right now. Sometimes we might meditate by drawing our attention to specific things, such as our breathing, a flower or a candle, or the act of walking. In Western applications, these types of meditation are often guided by a teacher or a recording. As we begin to take a look at these ideas of meditation, I invite you to consider that willingness and practice will help open your awareness and get you in touch with the present moment and that no spiritual beliefs, mystical assumptions, or magical thinking is involved.

One of the pioneers of this work is the Massachusetts Institute of Technology (MIT)–trained molecular biologist Jon Kabat-Zinn, who is also a student of the Zen master Seung Sahn. Over the past twenty years, Jon has made a major contribution to Western health care by combining his knowledge of Buddhism with his knowledge of Western biology and by developing ways to teach meditation and other skills in Western medical contexts. Originally, Kabat-Zinn was interested in how he could help people with chronic pain and terminal illness, for whom conventional medicine had little further to offer. He found that if people learned to shift into a focused, flexible, and nonjudgmental mode of awareness, and were able to remain in the presence of their discomfort or fear with a gentle and open-hearted acceptance, their pain often became more bearable and their lives more livable. Kabat-Zinn went on to help develop mindfulness-based stress reduction (MBSR), a program for people suffering from chronic physical illness and pain conditions.[5]

Research now supports the idea that MBSR and similar techniques can help us cope not only with physical pain but also with difficult feelings and challenging experiences and can help patients reduce their experience of stress and anxiety. The concepts of mindfulness and acceptance are now part of a new range of therapies, such as ACT,[6] DBT, mindfulness-based cognitive therapy (MBCT), and CFT. My website, mindfulcompassion.com, is a good place to start if you want to find out more about these therapies.

AN INTRODUCTION TO MINDFULNESS

The core of many of these newer approaches in psychotherapy is known as mindfulness, which is important to the development of compassion and refers to a 2,500-year-old method for training the mind to cultivate a particular way of paying attention.

Cultivating mindfulness can help make us aware of just how much our minds and our attention float around on the currents of different feelings and desires. When you sit quietly for a moment, allow your breath to find its own rhythm and pace, rest in that breath, and let your mind settle into the experience of breathing, you'll notice that your mind quickly moves away from the focus on your breathing and turns to other things. For example, you may start to think about what you need to do tomorrow, what to make for dinner, or what Aunt Ethel said about your new dress. This is sometimes called "automatic pilot" or "monkey mind." It's completely natural and relates to our always-on, "better safe than sorry" problem-solving machine and threat-detection system, which is easily activated and which can dominate our behavior, direct our attention, and seize control of our consciousness. After all, that's what it's designed to do.

Mindfulness is a way of noticing how our attention gets pulled in different directions, and it's a way of practicing the gentle, persistent art of returning our attention to the present moment. Mindfulness training has been demonstrated to be an effective treatment for a range of psychological problems, such as depressive relapse, anxiety, and emotion-regulation difficulties.[7] By developing our ability to be mindful, and by learning how to apply mindfulness to more healthy methods of coping with stress, we may become able to change our habitual and unhelpful responses to anxiety.[8]

If you've ever had to walk in a forest on a cool and cloudy night without even moonlight to guide you, you may understand what it is like to be truly in the dark. The trees obscure whatever light there is. All around you, the limits of your vision give way to blackness that may cause you to occasionally freeze in your tracks or nervously feel your way forward. The uncertainty of this sensory void might narrow your behavior and severely restrict the ways in which you feel comfortable moving. The limited perception may be thrilling and challenging, or it may be frightening and debilitating.

What if you could see in the dark? Not with a flashlight, but by possessing a kind of infrared vision that would allow you to see a richer palette of colors than you could have imagined. You could run and hurdle your way through the forest the way you might on a bright, calm spring day. Your actions would be your own again. No more feeling around in the dark.

We discussed in chapter 2 how our minds have evolved the capacity to relate one experience to any other experience. This capacity weaves everything we have ever known into a web, in which one thought or emotion may ceaselessly trigger another. When they unfold before us, we experience these thoughts and emotions as if they were real and true, and this allows the random associations of our imagination to seize control of our feelings and behaviors and, in fact, of our lives. We have also discussed how the more we try to push our thoughts and feelings away, the stronger they become.

However, our ability to clearly see the world around us, with all of its possibilities and meanings, is obscured by the content of our minds, much as our vision is obscured by the dark that surrounds us in the forest. Our range of available behaviors narrows as we grope around, treading carefully. We become enveloped and enshrouded by the uncertainty of our futures, the regrets of our past, and the ceaseless struggle to rid ourselves of pain and suffering due to our anxiety.

But, again, what if we could see in the dark? Not by changing the contents of our thoughts or by altering our internal environment; nor by dispelling the dark, the experience of pain, the universality of human suffering, or the finitude of life; but by cultivating the capacity to see clearly by being open and able to feel things for what they are.

We broaden our possibilities as we become more able to see through the darkness and rid ourselves of our attachment to our own past stories or the way we've judged ourselves. We become more able to move with more freedom through our lives, with passion, dignity, and abandon, toward what matters most to us, as freely as we could move through the forest on a bright spring day.

FROM MINDFULNESS TO COMPASSION: CFT

Along with mindfulness, one of the other great traditions of the East is the deliberate development of compassion for all living beings. The Dalai Lama points out that compassion can quite literally transform our minds.[9]

We discussed earlier how compassion from other people has a calming effect on us: when we're upset because of frightening or saddening circumstances, we turn to our partners or friends for help, support, and attention. They listen carefully, validate our feelings, and make it clear that they'll do what they can to help. We become secure in the knowledge that they care about what happens to us, that they're not condemning us, and that they're kind. How does this make you feel? But how would you feel if you asked for help from someone you care about and she seemed quite dismissive and disinterested, not only by what she said but also by her body language? What if she gave you the distinct impression that she might even blame or judge you for having such problems in the first place?

We all have an intuitive wisdom that loving-kindness, support, and compassion help us to bear our suffering and that criticism, neglect, shaming, and blaming usually make things much worse. This is true of self-criticism as well!

Many years ago, my friend and colleague Paul Gilbert, clinical psychologist and researcher, noticed that some of his clients became very self-critical or ashamed when they were distressed: they were good at kicking themselves when they were down. Paul found that he couldn't always help them by challenging their negative thinking or by teaching them mindfulness; however, when he taught them to be kind to themselves, he could often help them move away from their focus on self-condemnation. Some people were afraid of being kind to themselves and feared any form of self-compassion; however, even when we've learned to be distrustful of the concept of compassion, such as when our caregivers have been abusive or neglectful, mind training can help us unlearn this notion and can begin to free us from anxiety and destructive emotions.

Paul was inspired to develop a form of compassionate mind training based on his observations and his understanding of inherent biological soothing processes that can create a new relationship with anxiety and with shame and self-criticism. Self-compassion can allow us room to feel the pain and complexity of our emotions, which we may need to confront so that our anxiety loosens its grip. This may be painful, and complicated, but when we develop a basic orientation to be helpful, supportive, kind, and accepting toward ourselves, we may be able to deal with, and more importantly, tolerate, our distress better and have more control over the direction of our behavior and our lives. The compassion-focused therapy approach to anxiety is based on this idea.

Compassion involves more than just kindness. The Dalai Lama defines compassion as a sensitivity to the suffering of others, with a commitment to do something about it. He points to two key elements: attention (sensitivity) and motivation (commitment). The approach to compassion we'll develop here incorporates these insights. We should also note that over 2,600 years ago, the teacher known as the Buddha ("Buddha" is Sanskrit for "The One Who Woke Up") talked in terms of an eightfold path for the cultivation of compassion involving attention, thinking, speech, livelihood, and action. Developing scientific approaches to the cultivation of compassion is fundamental to compassion-focused therapy (CFT) and compassionate mind training. CFT involves the therapeutic relationship and a way of thinking about psychological problems; compassionate mind training refers to specific exercises that anybody can use to train the mind to develop compassionate qualities.

CFT is linked to Buddhist approaches to mindfulness; for example, in the Mahayana tradition, compassion is seen as having a central transformational power, and Mahayana trains people in particular kinds of attention, thinking, feeling, and behavior to help them transform their experiences of such events as anxiety. CFT shares part of this approach, in that specific methods are used to bring about changes in attention, emotions, and compassionate action. However, unlike traditional Buddhism, CFT is also based on evolutionary psychology and neuroscience.

When Paul Gilbert was developing his therapeutic techniques, he noticed that shame and self-criticism were often triggered by experiences of anxiety and distress, and these feelings and attitudes interfered with his patients' ability to move toward their goals in therapy. As a result, one of the central aims of CFT is to help people address the shame and blame they may heap on themselves in response to anxiety and distress. CFT emphasizes that we've emerged from an evolutionary process, as a part of the flow of life on this planet. We didn't choose to be here; we didn't choose our families, the cultures we were born into, or the many elements of our history that have shaped who we are. In a very real sense, who we've become and what we're experiencing isn't our design and, again, is not our fault; however, it's important to not give up and collapse into a heap but to see this as the beginning of moving toward a fuller understanding of ourselves and taking responsibility for our lives. We have the ability to think about and make decisions about how we want our minds to be developed—in the same way we make decisions about how we develop and train our bodies. If we never exercise and if we eat whatever we want whenever we feel like it, we'll become overweight and unhealthy. But knowing this gives us the option to learn about our diet and the importance of exercise. It's the same with our minds: knowing how tricky they are, and how sensitive to anxiety, gives us the option to learn how to cope with anxiety. We may choose to take responsibility for the course of our lives, but also we must bear in mind that suffering is a universal part of the human condition—anxiety is a natural and unavoidable part of human experience. If we're worried, agitated, panicked, or desperate, we can take some comfort in remembering that it's not our fault. By doing so, we can see anxiety as a natural part of our design and then learn that we can respond to our anxiety by taking a mindful and accepting mental stance. Instead of habitually responding to anxiety in ways that can actually make things worse, such as trying to suppress our experiences, abusing drugs and alcohol, or adopting a self-critical attitude, we can respond by doing things that will help us cope.

CREATING INNER COMPASSION AND THE ATTACHMENT SYSTEM

The CFT model is based on research showing that some of the ways in which we instinctively regulate our response to threats have evolved from the attachment system that operates between infant and mother and from other basic relationships between mutually supportive people. We have specific systems in our brains that are sensitive to the kindness of others, and the experience of this kindness has a major impact on the way we process these threats and the way we process anxiety in particular.

Two of the most significant twentieth-century psychologists, John Bowlby and Mary Ainsworth, observed that the attachment bond between a caregiver and an infant provides more than just protection, feeding, and learning opportunities. It also provides what's known as a secure base, a soothing and calming potential retreat from distressing emotions or environmental threats. This secure base is one aspect of our behavior that has been passed down to us through evolution, and it has served us well. It's natural for us to turn to emotionally significant people in our lives, and even to our internal representations of them, when we feel threatened, agitated, or overwhelmed. In the 1980s, Paul Gilbert became interested in the internal mechanisms that help us feel safe and the way these feelings of safety interact with feelings associated with threat. He understood that if children and adults were able to be calmed by the presence of supportive or caring others, there had to be a direct link between support and the experience of threat. So, after much research, he labeled our physiological system that switches on these feelings of safety "the social-safeness system." The social-safeness system involves a responsiveness to our significant attachment figures—specifically, to their accessibility or proximity and to certain communicative behaviors, such as their facial expression, tone of voice, and touch. The activation of attuned, secure, soothing relationships allows us to interact with our environment with greater confidence when we face challenges, because we know we can return to a sense of safety and protection in this secure base when necessary. Thus there's a connection between feeling safe and being able to explore. This is important because, as we'll see, there's a close interaction between mindfulness, which allows you to have open and explorative attention, and a feeling of safety.

The process of establishing a secure base and attachments involves a special set of brain cells known as mirror neurons, which allow us to literally feel what other people are feeling when we observe their behavior. According to Daniel Goleman, mirror neurons "act as a neural Wi-Fi, attuning to the other person's internal state moment to moment and recreating that state in our own brain—their emotions, their movements, their intentions. This means [that such a feeling as] empathy is based not just on reading the external signs of someone else's feeling, like the hint of a frown, or the irritation in their voice. Because of mirror neurons, we feel with the other. Empathy, then, includes attuning to our own feelings in order to better sense what's going on with the other person."[10]

According to attachment theory, secure relationships with others allow us to better cope with and manage the range of difficult emotions that arise in response to inner and outer circumstances. When we're threatened, our attachment system is activated and we seek to be close to and gain comfort from a significant person in our lives. This sort of relationship is referred to as an attachment relationship. The person who's the object of attachment—who may help us cope with the perceived threats and access our positive emotions—is sometimes referred to as an attachment figure.

Of course, there are differences from person to person in how effectively, or consistently, this attachment system functions. Those of us raised with stable, secure attachment relationships are more likely to be resilient, be flexible, and have an increased capacity to cope with difficult emotions.[11] Those of us who experience neglect, trauma, abuse, or even just a generally inconsistent and emotionally unavailable attachment relationship to our caregiver are more likely to have difficulty coping, being reflective and thoughtful, and soothing ourselves. A person who can activate, even symbolically, her attachment and affiliation system to respond to difficult emotions may have an easier time with self-compassion. Studies suggest that a person who has a secure attachment system may focus more of her attention and resources on generating positive emotions, on problem-solving, or on shifting her perspective on events than would a person with an unreliable, anxious, or avoidant style of attachment.[12]

Additionally, and on the biological side, we have certain hormones, such as oxytocin, that are linked to affiliation[13] and that help us downgrade threat processing, in the ways kindness and self-compassion can soothe us when we're fearful. When we practice self-compassion for long periods, it seems that regions of the brain that involve self-soothing and positive emotions are activated more easily, particularly in the face of stress;[14] thus, they help us cope with anxiety.

The key idea in using CFT to address anxiety is to specifically train our minds to focus on compassion and to activate compassionate ways of responding to our anxiety, in order to better regulate our feelings. By doing so, we're stimulating specific biological systems in our brains designed to calm down the threat-detection system. I can show you this with a simple diagram that we use in CFT.

If you worry too much or think about certain things over and over again, or if you're too self-critical, it will simply stimulate your threat-detection system and cause you to get locked in to stimulating your threat-response system. It's possible, though, to step out of that by redirecting your thoughts, redirecting your attention, or becoming mindful. The idea is to break the link between what your "new brain" is doing and your old-brain threat-detection system. Part of the essence of CFT is using parts of our minds, including the affiliation system, that have evolved with the specific purpose of calming down the threat-detection system. After all, there are direct connections between these two.

Basic evolved system in our brain

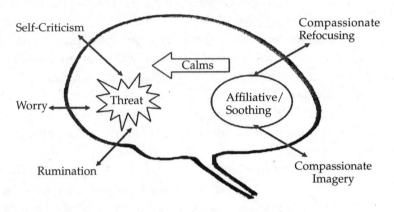

From *Compassion Focused Therapy: Distinctive Features*, Gilbert, 2010; reprinted with permission of Routledge.

Over the millennia, as societies have evolved and grown from isolated bands of kinfolk into sprawling, sophisticated civilizations, people's fears have shifted. While we need no longer fear many of the things our ancestors feared—modern society has reduced threats from natural predators, the occurrence of certain childhood diseases, and food shortages—we face an array of other types of threats. Early humans lived in small groups in which each person was familiar to the rest; today, we're often surrounded by strangers. We now also live in a world of constant social comparison in which we fear being seen as inferior. Early human child care was based on multiple caregivers, involving extended family members, such as grandmothers, siblings, and friends. This is less true today, when many families are smaller or living apart. In many areas of our lives, there's something of a mismatch between the environment that affected our evolution and the environment that surrounds us now; this increases our vulnerability to a whole range of anxieties. Our understanding of the reasons for this discord and subsequent increase in anxiety can facilitate social change. It can also help us understand that our vulnerability to anxiety is not our fault.

The location of my practice in the heart of New York City means that, in the middle of relative abundance and safety, I regularly meet people whose minds have conjured innumerable terrors. Thankfully, each of these clients possesses the wisdom of self-compassion and the ability to soothe herself, even if she's unaware of this inherent wisdom and ability. The process of training the mind to generate self-compassion, mindfulness, and acceptance will run throughout this book, and, hopefully, the act of bringing your intuitive wisdom into contact with your anxiety will open new possibilities in your life.

THE THREE-CIRCLE MODEL OF EMOTION REGULATION

Our brains and bodies have many different ways of regulating our emotional responses. For our purposes, we're going to look at three major systems that regulate our emotions and affect our response to what's going on around us. In CFT, these systems are often referred to using the three-circle model, representing three of the most important areas involved in human emotional response. The illustration below shows these three circles and how they interact:

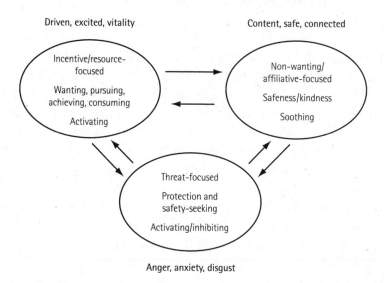

Three Types of Affect Regulation System

From Gilbert, 2009, *The Compassionate Mind*; reprinted with permission.

In the past thirty years or so, our understanding of how the brain creates and regulates emotion has advanced enormously. It has long been known that we have a system in our brains that enables us to detect and respond to threats.[15] What has become more evident recently is that we also have different types of positive emotion: one kind is associated with drive and achievement, doing and acquiring; another is associated with inner calmness and a sense of peaceful well-being. When we're not stimulating the drive and threat-detection systems—as everyday life does all the time—the mind settles and this second type of emotion can come through; these are linked to endorphins and such hormones as oxytocin, which may have evolved with the attachment system.

This is a simplified imagining of the neuroscience, but it's helpful to think about what we're trying to do with our brains when we practice compassion. Keep in mind that these systems are constantly interacting. It may be a good idea to think of them as if they were colors that were constantly mixing to create new colors, which, when applied to a canvas, can create different shapes, patterns, and balances. Let's look at these systems, or circles, in more detail.

The Threat-Detection and Safety-Seeking System

You've seen the ways the threat-detection and safety-seeking system can act on us to influence our attention, thinking, emotions, and behaviors and how we've evolved with the capacity to detect threats quickly. Activation of our threat-detection system doesn't require a direct threat to our well-being— it may also kick in if our loved ones or companions face danger. It also may be activated by social threats, such as separation from or rejection or abandonment by people in our family or social group, which can make us feel vulnerable to attack.

The brain's threat-detection system processes information gathered by the senses—sight, hearing, smell, taste, and touch—and when it perceives danger, it stimulates certain areas in the emotion-processing regions of the brain (the limbic system).[16] In particular, the amygdala, a cluster of nerve cells located on either side of the brain, becomes activated very rapidly, sending information to another part of the brain, the hypothalamus, which activates the stress response. The hypothalamus then communicates with the adrenal gland, and the body becomes ready for danger and starts to produce adrenaline and cortisol, a hormone released in response to stress. In an instant, we're ready for action.

Generally, this isn't a favorite circle for people to hang out in for pro-longed periods; however, if you've struggled with an anxiety disorder, this may feel all too familiar to you.

The Drive and Resource-Acquisition System

For a moment, imagine that an e-mail pops up on your computer or phone as you're reading this book. The e-mail is from your spouse or partner, informing you that the lottery ticket you bought together is a winner—on the order of hundreds of millions of dollars! In other words, you're instantly and fabulously wealthy. Can you imagine what that excitement would feel like coursing through your body, as you realized that all of your financial troubles had just evaporated and you thought of all the places you could visit—all the things you could buy? If you can, that rush and thrill rep-resents the activation of something called the incentive-focused emotion-regulation system. Our positive emotions, such as those that correspond to a sense of thrill or ecstasy, are involved in our seeking out those things that will help us survive or enhance our experience.[17] All the things we do for pleasure, such as searching for the perfect meal, the best vacation, or excit-ing sexual experiences, and our drive to win, to celebrate, and to revel in being alive, are all expressions of this system.

Although much of this may seem positive, it can also turn fairly nega-tive if the incentive-focused system becomes too dominant. For example, people who experience manic episodes can have their lives dominated by excessively expansive or related moods. Their sense of themselves can swell, and they can find themselves obsessively seeking out intense pleasure despite high risks. They may not be able to sleep, or they may become completely engulfed by goal-oriented pursuits. People with addictions may also face an overly active incentive-focused system. Under such conditions our thoughts can race, our impulses can be difficult to restrain, and our lives can feel unmanageable.

This system involves a neurochemical called dopamine,[18] which is related to our experience of being driven to do things. Many different human expe-riences involve an increase in dopamine, such as the intense experience of falling in love, or going to an all-night rave, or cheering as your team advances toward winning the World Series. Activation of dopamine is absolutely essential for human survival, but an overabundance can lead to problems.

The way we function does not involve one emotion-regulation system ruling the roost over the others, and our aim should be to achieve a better balance among these different emotion-regulation systems for flexible, healthy, and adaptive functioning.

The Social Safety and Soothing Systems

Some animals exhibit survival ability and a capacity to engage with their environment soon after birth. A newborn foal, for example, is shortly up and running, as if it already knew most of what it needed to know. But when we think of a human infant, unable to defend herself or even crawl for the first few months and absolutely dependent on her caregivers for survival, we can begin to understand how much help, protection, support, and guidance children need to help them develop their soothing and contentment system so they can go out to explore the world.

The hormone oxytocin is also involved in a feeling of happiness that arises when we feel safe, connected, and loved. The activation of compassion within ourselves is very much related to this soothing and contentment system.[19] If our threat-detection system evolved as a way for us to protect ourselves through defensive actions, then the soothing and contentment system has evolved as a way for us to protect ourselves through caring, kind, and supportive attachment bonds.[20] Our compassion for ourselves and others appears to emerge through the evolution of our affiliations, and our ability to regulate our emotions draws on our sense of safety, our contentment, and an awareness of our connection to others.

We're just beginning to understand the soothing and contentment system. What's our sense of contentment made of? Older psychological models of happiness, such as those derived from dear old Sigmund Freud, often looked at the reduction of our subconscious driving forces. Other models looked at the ways our threat-detection system could be tweaked, or schedules of simple rewards met to help us become satisfied; however, current research points us in another direction. It appears that we have a specific emotional system that allows us to experience peacefulness, contentment, and well-being. Certain states of mind allow the body to release neurochemicals that directly involve a sense of soothing. When we find ourselves in situations that activate these chemicals, such as when we're in the calming presence of a nurturing, wise, and beloved family member, our soothing and contentment system is directly utilizing neurochemistry that supports and enables these feelings. Far from a mere blissed-out warmth, the activation of the soothing and contentment system can involve a subjective sense of peacefulness, clarity of mind, and insight. This is not due to just an absence of anxiety and fear; it is also due to strong, moving, and potentially transformational experiences of positive emotions.

Compassionate mind training aims to help us focus on and then easily access our experiences of contentment, self-soothing, and safety. We can use many methods, ranging from visualization and meditation to changes in behavior that lead to greater self-care and cultivate our capacity for compassion. All of these methods involve the deliberate activation of the soothing and contentment system, which has evolved from the way mammals care for their young and from the emotional bond between parent and child.

As you probably know, the principle that underlies our understanding of evolution is natural selection, whereby the traits and behaviors that promote the survival and flourishing of a species tend to be passed from generation to generation, and those traits that don't lead to survival will die off. From this point of view, what are the evolutionary functions of the human behavior that we'd describe as "caring for one another"? Well, most obviously, caring for our young allows them the greatest chances of survival and of passing their own genetic code to subsequent generations. Beyond this, bonds among families, friends, and relatives have allowed human beings to form groups and cooperate to ensure the survival and well-being of the group. Emerging from these behaviors are friendship, empathy, and altruism.

The way this happened was that, among mammals, the emotional systems related to soothing and contentment, which communicate safety, began to take on new functions that weren't present earlier in evolutionary history; the functions of experiencing affection, affiliation, and care; producing a sense of calm; and quieting our threat-detection system.

When we view the evolution of caregiving and its relationship to the soothing and contentment system, it makes sense that because mammals have fewer offspring than many other kinds of animals, it's far more important that these offspring survive. You might see evolution as life playing out myriad options, exploring and evolving different ways to flourish and grow, in ever more complex and efficient ways. When Paul Gilbert describes evolution as a flow of life, he's being far more than poetic. There was a literal, physical transformation of the raw material of life on Earth into amino acids, proteins, and DNA, then into the variety of species that gave birth to one another, survived, and changed over hundreds of millions of years.

Mammalian parents care for and invest in their young, providing the "secure base" we mentioned earlier, which allows offspring to safely explore their environment and then return to a protected, secure base. And with the arrival of primates, and eventually humans, with their caregiving behaviors, there emerged the soothing function of the attachment bond between the caregiver and child that serves as the foundation for the "compassionate mind": human caregiving emerged as a complex blend of emotions, motivations, and behavioral tendencies that result in social mentalities with effects that are unique to humans.

CONTEMPORARY AND ANCIENT CONCEPTS OF COMPASSION

The concept of compassion is found incorporated into the earliest writings— for example, the Rig Veda, a beautiful epic poem from Central Asia composed perhaps more than 10,000 years ago. When great civilizations emerged to transform people's way of life, lifting them out of subjugation and oppression and creating abundance and prosperity, the shift involved a movement toward compassion and interpersonal empathy.[21] The roots of the world's great religions and traditions of wisdom, such as Christianity, Judaism, Islam, Hinduism, and particularly Buddhism, have emphasized compassion as a source of the alleviation of suffering. Western science has now come to recognize compassion's role in society and its involvement in our emotional well-being: compassion has an evolutionary purpose, an essentially human character, and a measurable effect on the human mind and body.

All of us want pleasant feelings and, conversely, wish to rid ourselves of pain, displeasure, and anxiety. That just makes sense. But what's the value of soothing above and beyond just feeling good? What purpose might this ability to regulate our emotions through mindful compassion serve? One key purpose is to give us courage, without which we wouldn't be able to put into action what's needed to calm and soothe ourselves, to confront our demons both inside us and outside. The loving parent keeps the child out of danger but also encourages the child to face up to the challenges of the world by learning how to experience anxiety and deal with it. So, compassion is intimately linked to courage and the ability to face up to the things we fear. And you can find that courage within yourself more easily if you create a calm, understanding, and encouraging voice in your head. That's the simple message: if you train your mind to be compassionate, you'll allow yourself the space to be able to do those things you need to do in order to deal with your anxiety.

I ask you now to use your imagination to notice how compassion and mindfulness might serve a broader purpose: Imagine that you're the captain of a sailing vessel, and night has fallen on another day of your voyage. It might as well be ancient times, because you have no navigational instruments—no GPS, no compass, no sextant—and the crew rely on your keen eyes and your sense of direction to guide the ship. Imagine that you're sailing this ship toward whatever it is that you value most in your life—you saw it at last light, just on the horizon—that aim that will allow you to feel fulfilled, purposeful, and vital. Whatever that is for you, right here and now, is waiting on that horizon. You're confident the ship is seaworthy; over the years, you've seen just how much stress and strain she can withstand. Nevertheless, tonight the sea is churning. All around you dark clouds and white-capped waves are swirling, and a storm threatens. This storm is your anxiety. The waves grow large, and the ship begins to pitch frighteningly. The crew shouts warnings and fearful cries to you, just as you can envision for yourself various horrible possible consequences of shipwreck. You are entering the storm of your anxiety. How can you remain calm enough to sail this ship on through to what matters most to you? If you turn back, you turn away from a life well lived. Though the storm seems to threaten to engulf the ship, you choose to carry on. Right here and right now, you can choose to bring your full, flexible, and focused attention to the present moment, through the practice of mindful awareness. Just as you, the captain, love your ship and crew and put their well-being before your own and can steel your determination, so too can you access a great wellspring of care and acceptance for yourself, through training your compassionate mind. In time, you can learn to activate your intuitive wisdom, access your mindful compassion, and remain calm in the storm of anxiety, as you move forward in the direction of your own valued aims.

This ability to remain calm in the storm is not only available to you, but is designed to be an essential part of what it means to be human. Many people have been aware of this for a long time and, fortunately, they have recorded a log of their own voyages and left a course for us to follow.

As we approach a deeper understanding of the role of compassion in emotion regulation, let's take a look at what Western psychologists and scientists have to say about the situation. Compassion's essence can be found in basic human kindness, with a deep awareness of the suffering of oneself and of other living beings, coupled with a wish and an effort to relieve this suffering. This definition lays the groundwork for CFT, and research has found that training people in developing a compassionate mind in a gradual, structured way can reduce depression, help lessen shame and self-criticism, and help patients deal with difficult emotions, such as anxiety.

Compassion is not just an emotion; it's also a multipurpose system and strategy for functioning and interacting with the world. Many aspects of being human, such as thinking, the experience of emotions, overt behaviors, and the deployment of attention, are all coordinated and activated by compassion in what CFT refers to as a social mentality,[22] which is a blend of thoughts, emotions, and actions that guide our motivation. Social mentalities also direct and affect our attention, thoughts, and behaviors as we seek out and maintain relationships with others and are involved in the positive feelings that arise when our relationships are working for us. They are also involved, however, in our experience of negative emotions that show up when our relationships aren't working.

ARCHETYPES AND SELF-COMPASSION

The idea of an archetype has its origins in the writings of the psychiatrist Carl Jung, who defined archetypes as representing innate frameworks and prototypes for understanding ourselves and our environment. These prototypes might not exist in the forefront of our awareness, but they influence us nevertheless, via our unconscious, to inform our thoughts, feelings, and behaviors. Examples are the prototype of "the mother" and "the hero." Across cultures, languages, social structures, and historical periods, such prototypes emerge in myth, in social roles, and in the stories we make up in our own minds about the world. Archetypes represent "the source of the repeating desires and relationships that echo down through history."[23] But social mentality, which we touched on earlier, demystifies the concept of the archetype by viewing such patterns as naturally selected strategies that have evolved to guide our feelings, thoughts, and behaviors toward the best way to adapt and interact with our environment. So, when we're training ourselves to cultivate our minds to be compassionate, we're actually activating and then developing an innate social mentality.

Another leading Western researcher on compassion, Kristin Neff, has emphasized a theory of "self-compassion,"[24] which is different from either self-esteem or compassion for others. Self-compassion involves three primary elements: self-kindness, awareness of our common humanity, and mindful awareness. It has been shown that higher levels of self-compassion have been found to correlate with lower levels of depression and anxiety. Such research has also demonstrated positive correlations between self-compassion and a range of other desirable experiences, such as enhanced life satisfaction, feelings of social connectedness, a sense of personal initiative, and other positive emotions.[25]

It has been suggested that we've evolved to be able to preserve both ourselves and our genetic relatives and that we may have different emotional systems that guide our own survival and the survival of humanity as a group. The species-preservation emotion system is thought to have evolved from the loving bond between the nurturing mother and the dependent children, who were more likely to survive under the care and attention of loving and dedicated parents than under the care of neglectful or inadequate parents. Over millions of years, those qualities of nurturing, kindness, and care gradually emerged as central and essential to our survival. As a result, we've evolved to feel soothed and feel safe in the presence of kindness, care, and loving attention. In turn, our sense of compassion has evolved into one of the major systems we use to regulate our emotions.

BUDDHIST MODELS OF COMPASSION

While Western thinkers adopted an outward-looking perspective, crafting technologies and scientific methods that would influence our physical, outer dimensions of interaction with the environment, Eastern thinkers devoted generations of effort to mapping and understanding the inward-looking perspective of mental and emotional experience. Only a few years ago, the very idea that reliable, scientific solutions to psychological problems might emerge from spiritual tradition may have sounded ludicrous to many psychologists and laypeople alike; however, scientific data continues to prove that Buddhist psychology has produced effective ways for us to alleviate human suffering, not only by altering our behavior and emotions, but also by actually changing the function and structure of the human brain itself.[26] So, when we turn to Buddhist psychology as a starting point in understanding the nature of compassion, we turn to it with a confident knowledge that thousands of years of scholarship and meditative practice have provided us with a legacy of unparalleled wisdom about the nature of our minds and our emotions.

Buddhist psychology expounds the idea that we all live our lives through the veil of our own imagination, thoughts, feelings, and emotional memories and that, as much as we might strive to see things as they really are, our inner world filters and distorts our perception. The aim of Buddhist psychology is to train the mind to experience reality as directly and clearly as possible, moment by moment. In doing so, and in coming to accept reality just as it is, we can take a broader view of reality and become less attached to and stuck within our pain and suffering.

Generations of Buddhists have asserted that central to our individual spiritual evolution are four aspects of compassion, known as *metta*, *karuna*, *mudita*, and *upekkha*.[27] Let's take a look at each of these in some depth.

Metta refers to a feeling of loving-kindness for ourselves and for others—a warm, friendly, and loving feeling; it means that we aspire for happiness, both for ourselves and for others. This particular concept is crucial to an important and widely practiced meditation based on cultivating just this quality of *metta*. Later we'll look at this technique in some depth, and you'll learn exactly how you can cultivate this quality for yourself.

Buddhist meditators have long believed that a gradual development of *metta* is essential to our well-being and personal evolution. Recently, there have been some exciting studies that seem to support this view using neuroimaging to examine the brain functions and structures of long-term practitioners of compassion meditation.[28] It has been shown that advanced, compassion-focused meditators respond to distressing images and events with an increased activation of brain regions involved in empathy, love, and positive emotions. This supports Paul Gilbert's assertion that compassionate mind training can result in a shift in our method of emotion regulation from reliance on the threat-focused response system to the affiliative, compassion-oriented soothing system. It appears that regular practice in developing loving-kindness may actually relate to changes in the brain that can help us deal better with stress and difficult emotions.

Karuna is typically translated directly as "compassion" and involves a heartfelt aspiration for all beings to be free from suffering. Beyond this aspiration or motivation, *karuna* relates to the clarification of compassion as a value that guides and informs our behavior. People who are cultivating *karuna* are engaged in an ongoing commitment to ethical behavior that serves the value of compassion and leads to happiness being shared and nurtured. As a result, those practicing *karuna* engage in a process related to actively bearing the suffering of others; indeed, modern behavioral research has found that simply acknowledging that we can feel each other's pain is crucial to our ability to be more sympathetic and understanding. An element of *karuna* will be involved in your work to train your mind to be more compassionate.

Mudita describes a sense of joy that arises when we appreciate the well-being and happiness of others, and it's believed to be an inexhaustible source of inner happiness that can be accessed through mental training. In some Buddhist teaching sources, *mudita* is related to the feeling of deep happiness that parents take in the flourishing of their children. Jealousy, envy, and the addictive pursuit of pleasure are considered to be the opposites of *mudita*, and activation of these emotions is seen as a block to the experience of *mudita*. The goals of developing *mudita* relate to the goals of CFT, which aims to teach us how to deliberately come into contact with a sense of compassion in order to regulate other, destructive emotions.

Upekkha, which is discussed in the earliest texts of classical Buddhist psychology, is most directly translated as "equanimity," an ability to meet both the good and the bad in life with an attitude of acceptance, willingness, calmness, and understanding. Just such an attitude of mindful acceptance and a willingness to embrace the whole of life, from the smooth to the rough, has emerged in the most advanced research in psychotherapy as an essential element in the process of emotional healing. As we begin to learn about training our compassionate mind, we'll see how cultivating acceptance of things just as they are enables us to experience joy and freedom more readily.

These four elements are the building blocks of human happiness; however, there's one more aspect of the Buddhist concept of compassion that I'd like to discuss: *bodhicitta*.[29]

Bodhicitta is usually referred to as a passionate and selfless desire for the end of suffering of all beings; however, I like to remember what the roots of the word mean. "Bodhi" means "waking up," and "citta" means "mind." Many practitioners of Mahayana Buddhism believe that regular practice of gentle yet disciplined mental training will result in the possibility that all beings can be free from suffering and that this possibility is a natural part of our waking up to the reality of the human condition. *Bodhicitta* relates to the wisdom of knowing how we are all deeply interconnected.

5

The First Turning of the Wheel of Compassion: Exploring the Attributes and Skills of the Compassionate Mind

CONTRASTING THE ANXIOUS MIND AND THE COMPASSIONATE MIND

In our earlier discussion we learned how anxiety affects our attention, thinking, behavior, emotions, imagination, and motivation. We also learned that our affiliation and compassion system can be activated to stimulate our compassionate mind and change our mental state so that we have a calmer and more soothing way to deal with our experiences, good or bad.

The diagrams below illustrate that two different types of brain patterns—the "threatened mind" and the "compassionate mind"—can affect the way we respond. Let's look at how the activation of your threatened mind might result in a different experience than the activation of your compassionate mind. Imagine that you've had a history of feeling anxious in social situations, and you're heading off to your first day of college, which starts with an orientation. All this week you'll be meeting new people and be expected to form new relationships, ask questions, and start conversations; basically you'll be faced with a host of different social challenges. This is the sort of thing you've dreaded your entire life, but it's something you have to face today. Your threat-detection system is already active and creating a state of anxiety, worry, and fear; you could hardly sleep last night.

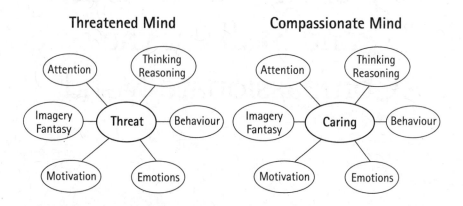

From Gilbert, 2010, *Overcoming Depression*; reprinted with permission.

Your threat-detection system will affect what you *attend to* in your environment; for example, you might scan the faces of the people at the orientation to see whether there's any evidence of disapproval. Your threatened mind might focus on hypothetical situations in which you embarrass yourself or say the wrong thing. Your attention might become fixed on past social experiences that have led to feelings of humiliation or rejection. The activation of your threat-detection system narrows your attention, narrows what you attend to, and keeps you feeling anxious.

But if you were to activate your compassionate mind, you'd deploy your attention differently. Yes, you might be focused partly on some feelings of anxiety; however, your compassion would allow you to mindfully make space for this and remember that these feelings are a natural part of the human condition and not your fault. The compassionate mind allows us to be kind to ourselves, and truly wish the best for ourselves, which then allows us to feel an inner sense of safety that gives us an ability to face uncertainty. In this example, instead of focusing on the negative "what ifs"—*What if that person doesn't like me? What if I spill my drink on my shirt and make a fool of myself?*—your attention may turn itself instead to the likely possibility that the experience of meeting new people will be rewarding and informative. Instead of putting pressure on yourself to perform, excel, and impress, you could allow yourself to be good enough, just as you are, in this very moment. This warm self-regard and acceptance might allow you to see your freshman orientation for what it is: a learning opportunity and a new beginning.

The threatened mind affects how you think and reason; it generates a range of worries and predictions about how badly things could go, because it's working in "better safe than sorry" mode.

Likewise, the compassionate mind affects how you think and reason— but in a different way, open more to opportunities than to fear of rejection. The compassionate mind provides a counterbalance to the threatened mind; it remembers that you aren't obliged to buy into the anxious thoughts that pop into your head.

If you let your threatened mind dominate, you may engage in certain behavior based on threat perception and a desire to find safety. So, in the example at hand, you may feel a desire to avoid the first day of college altogether and make up an excuse to stay at home. You may feel an urge to activate safety-seeking behavior, such as standing apart from the groups at orientation, pretending to look at your phone, avoiding eye contact, or even using sedatives or alcohol to "take the edge off." Your urge to avoid, escape, or push away your feelings of anxiety is a natural result of the stimulation of your threat-detection system, and it can be very hard to withstand the pull of such urges when you're stuck in threatened-mind mode.

In contrast, if you were to activate your compassionate mind in such a situation, new behavioral possibilities might present themselves. Remember: compassion gives us courage. As you made an effort to shift from your threatened mind to your compassionate mind, you might find the strength and wisdom to face your fear with mindfulness and acceptance and to more deeply engage in social interactions and new experiences. Rather than looking for ways to escape, you might focus on how to begin conversations, ask questions, and forge new relationships.

The compassionate mind invokes feelings of warmth and support—it may cause you to feel as though a dear friend and mentor is with you, guiding you toward opportunities to live in meaningful ways, and, although you're entering new and unfamiliar situations, with the help of your friend you can feel confident and secure that you can meet the challenge and handle your happy and sad emotions with equal measure.

Both the threatened-mind mode and the compassionate mind can also influence your motives, which would be different if you were faced with a consequence of danger than if you're faced with the reward of happiness and contentment. To return to our example, you may feel conflicted if on the one hand you value the potential good things that may result from college life but on the other hand avoid becoming involved in college life because of your anxiety.

The compassionate mind motivates you to be kind to yourself, to be aware of our common humanity, and to allow yourself to enjoy the present, moment by moment. The compassionate mind is, above all, motivated to help you cope with and maybe over time even alleviate your suffering. The *motive* of the compassionate mind during the freshman orientation is to gently and kindly support you as you face new challenges and take new risks, so that you might live a more fulfilled and meaningful life. Your secure base, your affiliation, is within you, and when you find this place of safety you can then courageously move toward your aims, your horizon.

ATTRIBUTES OF THE COMPASSIONATE MIND

Compassionate mind training employs the use of the different aspects of who we are. For example, we can build our ability to mindfully observe our thoughts and emotions with acceptance, without condemning ourselves for the way we feel, and with a sense of perspective on why we feel as we do. We can then choose to take care of ourselves, as best we can, through compassionate behavior. Compassionate mind training involves the development of attributes and skills that, combined, help us prepare to meet the challenges of anxiety. Compassion serves as a means of bringing our emotional systems into balance and increases our sense of well-being.

In CFT we use the concept of the compassionate mind because compassion is a mind-organizing process that brings together our motives, emotions, ways of thinking, and ways of paying attention.

The circular diagram below illustrates the different aspects of the compassionate mind. In the inner ring are the core attributes of compassion, and in the outer ring are the skills we can practice to develop our capacity for compassion.

Different Aspects of Compassionate Mind Training

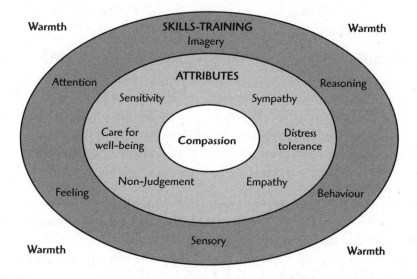

From Gilbert, *The Compassionate Mind*, 2009; reprinted with permission.

Your journey around the circle begins by exploring the attribute described in this diagram as "Care for well-being," which represents a compassionate *motivation* to care for ourselves and others and, as a result, to be motivated to address our problems with anxiety.

First, you must acknowledge that your struggle with anxiety is excessively distressing and may be holding you back from a life that is calmer or more content. Second, you must acknowledge that your life can be better if you come to terms with anxiety. After all, what would be the point of learning to manage your anxiety if it wouldn't improve the quality of your life?

To get in touch with your motivation, you might begin by writing down the benefits of working on your anxiety. If you wish, stop now and make a list of what you'd like to do if your anxiety weren't the focus of your attention. What have you given up due to the struggle with anxiety? Start with small things, and move on to bigger things. This list will help you to keep your aims in life—those important things on the horizon—in the forefront of your mind and may help you remember what motivates you.

Jennifer, whom we met earlier in this book, made this list for herself:

- "If I were less focused on anxiety, I could pay more attention to developing new relationships and making new friends."

- "If anxiety were less of a problem for me, I could explore new job opportunities rather than be stuck in one place."

- "If I were more willing to allow myself to experience anxiety without also worrying about it so much, and to hold myself in higher regard and be kinder to myself, perhaps I could ride out the waves of panic that show up when I have a panic-stricken anxiety attack. They usually last only a couple of minutes, and they don't cause me harm, but I can lose hours and sometimes days by anticipating and then worrying about whether I'll have one."

Consider the kinds of things that might get in your way—maybe you have thoughts that your anxiety is simply too great or too difficult to overcome. Your brain will be acting on both fronts—to motivate you to face your anxiety and to motivate you not to. The compassionate mind approach suggests that you take a kind, understanding view of this conflict within you and then, as best as you're able, begin to think about small steps first.

Motivation waxes and wanes, but it doesn't come out of the blue. To keep yourself motivated, it's useful to reflect on what you're willing to work for, suffer discomfort for, or climb mountains for. You see, all of us have our mountains to climb, and anxiety might be yours. Tuning in to your goals and those things worth working for can help you stay motivated to engage with your pain, fears, and anxiety—and then you'll know that you have, in your own way, been developing your courage.

When we're motivated to change something in our lives, or in ourselves, we may often have mixed feelings; for example, some time ago, I made a decision to lose some weight. I was able to connect with a desire to be healthier, to feel more energy, and to generally feel better about the way I looked. Still, there was a part of me that was unhappy about this proposed new course of action. My attachment to eating fresh pasta and homemade chocolate-chip cookies resulted in some serious mixed feelings about denying myself the chance to eat what I wanted, when I wanted. But mixed feelings are natural, and pretending they aren't swirling around won't help. Ultimately, I found it helpful to make space for the whole range of my feelings about weight loss. I tried to befriend both my ambition to be healthier and my sense of deprivation and entitlement when dieting. The trick was to allow these mixed feelings to be there, without handing my behavior and my life over to them. As a result, I did wind up losing the weight I'd hoped to, but not without the occasional bit of chocolate or ravioli finding its way into my diet.

To fully realize your compassionate motivation and allow it to flourish, recognize that your aspiration to care for yourself may need to share space in your heart and mind with your anger, your anxiety, your peevishness, and your resistance to, and fear of, change. Rolling with this resistance and opening yourself to the totality of these different feelings is a necessary part of the awakening of compassionate motivation.

Another key aspect of the compassion circle is *sensitivity*, which means paying attention to the various things that trigger anxiety, paying attention to how anxiety is experienced in the body, sensing the emotions that accompany these physical sensations, and paying attention to the kinds of thoughts that come with the anxiety. Compassionate sensitivity doesn't just mean that we become increasingly reactive, but that we become increasingly flexible and able to respond as we become more intimately and acutely aware of the quality of how we experience things moment by moment. It means that our attention is more available and open to our difficulties and our response to them. As our compassionate sensitivity grows, we learn how to focus on and notice what anxiety is provoking in us or others.

It's easy to avoid or deny what we're experiencing, especially when we're anxious, but if you're going to be compassionate toward yourself and come to terms with your experience of suffering due to your anxiety, you need to train yourself to pay attention to the things that may be contributing to your difficulty and adopt a curious and open point of view.

This training can also teach you to notice what helps you deal with your anxiety. Of course, being out of the anxiety-provoking situation or engaging in various safety-seeking behaviors can temporarily reduce anxiety—but the aim is to "get better, not just feel better." You can learn to pay attention to things that will help you respond in truly helpful ways—maybe by noting how to breathe soothingly and rhythmically, or maybe by noticing what happens when you change your way of thinking to a more compassionate-minded approach. The more we practice something the more confident we become, and it may be useful if you note down the mini-steps you've taken to respond to your anxiety differently, such as when you respond positively to other people's smiles or kind words, or when you feel empowered by meeting new people, or even just one new person, at a party. When you notice what works for you in the face of anxiety, you can build on these things and expand your range of workable, useful responses.

The third attribute of the compassionate mind in the CFT model is described as *sympathy*, and it involves being open to, and directly emotionally touched by, the suffering of others and ourselves. Compassionate sympathy is our ability to be emotionally in tune with our anxiety so that we're not running away from it or denying it but instead feel sympathetic toward ourselves and moved by our distress so that we're motivated to do something about it. Sympathy stands in direct contrast to anger—to getting angry with ourselves or angry with our anxiety. It's the activation of our emotional system, the way we feel, in response to perceived pain, or even perceived joy in the flourishing of ourselves or someone else. Compassionate sympathy isn't the same thing as being frightened of your anxiety or pitying yourself for your anxiety. It's a kind sensitivity to distress. We have an understanding of how painful and distressing anxiety can be sometimes, and just as our heart goes out to others who suffer from anxiety, so, too, should we feel sympathetic toward ourselves and our own suffering.

If compassionate mind training allows us to become increasingly sensitive and sympathetic, it makes a great deal of sense that we'd aim to also develop *distress tolerance*, which involves learning how to tolerate our experience of anxiety without thinking that we must turn off our feelings or buy into our internal stories that tell us we can't bear it. Our sensitivity will allow us to notice thoughts and attitudes that might be pushing us away from compassionate distress tolerance—and instead give us the feeling that the distress is overwhelming, rather than just deeply unpleasant. In order to experience and adapt our responses to suffering in others and ourselves, we can develop the capacity to tolerate distress and remain in the presence of disturbing feelings without feeling overwhelmed.

Compassionate distress tolerance will allow you to experience your internal response to pain and suffering without surrendering your outward behavior to your distress. Although you may still experience discomfort, worry, and fear, you'll gradually develop the ability to tolerate these states and make choices about how you wish to act in the world.

You may often wish your anxiety would just go away, and perhaps you fantasize that therapy, pills, or meditation would immediately banish your apprehension and take you to a state of ongoing bliss. But this isn't how this life tends to unfold, no matter how psychologically minded, wise, or productive we might become. It may be a bit disheartening to discover that part of well-being involves learning how to tolerate distress, but be assured that the compassionate development of resilience, proceeding step by step, will provide you with new ways of responding that allow you to be less frightened and more able to cope.

There are many times in life when we must tolerate anxiety; for example, the first time you drove a car, maybe during a driving lesson, was probably rather frightening. Taking a major exam, such as a college entrance exam, could also be frightening. But despite your fear and anxiety, you may have tolerated such feelings because you had an incentive that if you made it through the challenging experience, the rewards would be good for you. Notice how this links to the things we explored in the motivation section. Learning distress tolerance helps keep us going in the direction of our valued aims. After all, those things that bring meaning and vitality to our lives are the reasons we're willing to engage with painful feelings. When you pass your driver's test, you gain freedom to come and go as you please; when you pass your entrance exams, you get to further your education and move your life in the direction that brings you fulfillment.

There's no point in tolerating things that aren't useful, however. If you're being pressured by your peers to do something that either you know is wrong or you feel completely uncomfortable with, your compassionate mind will help you to have the courage to say no. Likewise, when there are other aims that you wish to pursue but that seem difficult, your capacity for distress tolerance becomes an important strength. One of the great costs of anxiety is the degree to which our struggle with it devours our time and energy and keeps us away from more profound and rewarding activities. Perhaps you avoid job interviews because you fear you'll be rejected. Or you remain at home engrossed in worries rather than spending time with friends, seeking out new experiences, or building new relationships. Compassionate distress tolerance can help us live fuller lives.

Research has proven that people who have more positive and realistic beliefs about their ability to tolerate emotions are better able to respond flexibly to their experiences both good and bad, are more mindful of the present moment, are better able to make decisions, and are less prone to depression and anxiety.[1] In CFT, compassionate distress tolerance affords us the opportunity to experience difficult emotions and yet continue to move toward what matters most to us.

In our CFT model, *empathy* is the attribute of the compassionate mind that involves our capacity to think about, understand, and comprehend the suffering we encounter in the world. It relates to how we understand that we and others have motivations, emotions, desires, and fantasies that often underpin our behavior. It relates to our understanding that we and others are products of evolution and desire and that we feel similar things—we're not alien to each other. Empathy enables us to understand that we, and our values, desires, and emotions, are also products of our history, and the sources of our feelings (including anxieties) can be found both in our histories and in the present moment.

The processing of the emotional pain of others and ourselves is known as *compassionate empathy* and is linked to our ability to tolerate distress. Here's how it works: imagine that somebody tells you that your friend's mother has died. When you call your friend, he's crying, very distressed, and grief-stricken. Although you didn't know your friend's mother, you're able to appreciate the range and depth of your friend's emotional experience. You can feel his anxiety and grief as if you were experiencing it yourself. Your empathy allows you to imagine what's going through his mind and body. Compassionate empathy allows you to recognize what might be helpful to him: how you might hold him in kindness, connect with him through your speech, or offer practical help. Beyond any logical or problem-solving mode, your empathy allows you to sense this experience from your friend's perspective, to feel as he might feel, and to be moved by this awareness. Whereas your sympathy might want you to make things better for him—for the pain to just go away (and that's a compassionate and understandable desire)—your empathy helps you understand this isn't possible and that what he needs is someone who'll simply listen and who'll understand and validate his experience and feelings.

Empathy provokes curiosity and a desire to explore, engage with, and work to alleviate the suffering that we're in intimate contact with. Compassionate empathy involves the capacity for gaining perspective, the ability to discern and internally represent the mental experience of others so that we can better understand another's needs, aspirations, emotions, and concerns. Related to this is self-compassionate empathy, in which we direct the same feelings toward ourselves as you did for your friend whose mother died. It can enable you to think about your anxiety, understand what your anxiety is really about, and understand what it needs in order to settle. Empathy invites you to react with wisdom and kindness, even if that means simply to understand and validate your feelings.

As discussed, anxiety often involves the activation of shame and self-blame. Depression and other unpleasant states also often involve severe self-criticism, or a hostile and judgmental view of ourselves or others. Our internal critic often keeps a running commentary, judging which feelings are good and which are bad. Mindfulness, however, involves a suspension of these judgments and the capacity to view ourselves and others from a noncondemning and nonjudgmental perspective. The attribute of the CFT model of mindfulness known as *nonjudgment* is a willingness to experience whatever our minds present, without buying into or being ruled by negative self-judgment, self-criticism, or self-condemnation. Compassionate nonjudgment encourages us to experience our thoughts and feelings for what they are and allows us to connect with a central theme in CFT—that our thoughts, feelings, and behavioral urges are not our fault. Compassionate nonjudgment can help us cultivate the compassionate mind.

Indeed, each of the attributes described above is an element in the activation of your compassionate mind. These elements are interdependent and support each other: if one attribute weakens or lessens, then compassion may falter. Imagine compassion without the motivation to be caring and helpful or without the desire to be tolerant of distress or feel empathy.

With this in mind, sometimes we need to do more work on one attribute than on another. All of them can be expanded and strengthened by compassionate mind training specific to each attribute. The training allows us to shape new behaviors and capacities through small, consistent steps, in a gradual process. You can't rush the process; gaining or enhancing these capabilities simply takes some time.

COMPASSIONATE SKILLS

As you do the work that lies ahead, it's important to remember that you aren't pursuing compassion for some abstract reason. All of your work in compassionate mind training is in response to anxiety and is aimed at helping you build a greater sense of well-being and thus the freedom to take your life in the direction you want it to go. Training the compassionate mind develops such attributes as motivation, empathy, and distress tolerance, which can help you cope with your anxiety. There are three main areas of compassionate skill: compassionate attention, compassionate thinking, and compassionate behavior.

Compassionate Attention

Compassionate attention involves directing your awareness to events in your outer and inner environment and relates to the quality, the direction, and the object of your attention, which, as we'll see, can go a long way toward helping you respond to your anxiety. For a moment, let's return to my client Jennifer and imagine that she's experiencing a rushed and hurried day at school, under the pressure of deadlines and faculty politics. She might find herself so caught up in the flow of the demands of the workplace that her field of attention has been narrowed by stress and anxiety and has caused her to attend to negative predictions and hassles. She might be continually glancing at the clock and running on autopilot while her threat-detection system runs into the red. In contrast, though, imagine the same situation with Jennifer skillfully deploying mindful, compassionate attention to what's going on around her. She may still feel anxious and stressed; however, her compassionate attention allows her to tune in to her emotional awareness with acceptance and warmth, moment by moment, and in turn she notices some of the more positive and rewarding aspects of her work and reconnects with her purpose of helping to shape the lives of her very young students. Her active, compassionate awareness gives her the breathing room and working space to function more smoothly and calmly and helps her take care of herself, as much as she can, throughout the day. This quality and focus of attention will emerge as you develop the ability to engage and activate your emotion-regulation system to access your own place of safety, your own "affiliation," and provide a sense of acceptance, kindness, and a secure base from which to operate. Mindfulness training is an excellent way to cultivate compassionate attention in order to better access the calming wisdom of self-compassion.

Compassionate Thinking

If you struggle with anxiety, it's likely that the way in which you think isn't helpful to you, isn't workable in the long run, doesn't open up opportunities for you, and doesn't move you toward your goals and values. Instead, your thinking probably focuses on threats and takes you in repetitive cycles in which you get more anxious or worrisome and see your options closing down. Compassionate thinking involves widening your perspective and flow of thoughts, in tune with a compassionate way of being.

Compassionate thinking happens when you make a decision to note the kind of thoughts going through your mind, particularly those linked to threats. Then, you make the decision to see such thoughts for what they are: events in your mind. You may decide to pause, draw attention into the present moment through an awareness of your breathing, and ask yourself whether you need to buy into and surrender to your threatened-mind thinking or, rather, there might be a more workable, purposeful, and compassionate way to respond to your environment in the here and now.

Granted, sometimes it may be helpful to be accurate and clear about what's guiding your thinking; for example, if your anxiety involves fear of having a heart attack, then it's important to get the information about the difference between feelings of panic and the true signs of a cardiac arrest. However, compassion is key—you're directing your thinking to be helpful, and it may not be helpful to seek evidence for the accuracy or veracity of your fears. In fact, I've worked with many clients who've obsessively pored over the Internet to search for data about how likely it is that they'll die in a plane crash or become ill from microwave-oven radiation. The data serves only to stir up their anxiety. Sometimes "looking for the evidence" can get us caught in a loop of safety-seeking behavior that activates our threat-detection system and bounces us around on waves of fear and apprehension. Additionally, sometimes highly accurate thoughts might not be very useful in a given situation. We can revisit the example of trying to escape from a high floor of a burning building by climbing down the fire escape: although it might be accurate to think *If I fall, I might die*, this isn't going to help you make your way down. Instead, if you focus on making your way down the fire escape, albeit clinging on for dear life, you can also then focus on your grip and your footholds and, carefully as you can, ease your way down. This is a good example of what's meant by compassionate thinking, which comes from a position of encouragement, warmth, kindness, and understanding rather than from cold logic. Remember that the definition of compassion involves recognition of your anxiety and suffering and an aspiration to do something about it.

Sometimes people can be very good at recognizing that the anxiety they're experiencing is irrational when they look at the evidence; however, their thoughts might be along the lines of My *heart is racing and it's scaring me, but I'm fit and healthy and am not about to have a heart attack, so it's stupid of me to be frightened.* Here, being able to discern that you're experiencing anxiety rather than having a heart attack might give you a bit of relief, but the tone of condemnation and the desire to suppress the thoughts might actually be counterproductive. Unleashing your inner critic and trying to avoid your fears might have a semblance of rationality to it, but it's unlikely to help you deal with your threatened-mind mode. In fact, as you angrily tell yourself off, you might even stoke up the activity of your "fight, flight, or freeze" response by becoming irritable at perceived threats. Alternatively, if you access your compassionate mind, and your compassionate thinking, you can be more patient and understanding toward yourself and your fears. You can encourage yourself to face the fear, let it wash over you, then shift your focus to other, more positive things. Time and again we come back to this motivation to be helpful. The aim is for you to be supportive to yourself, whether it's by generating alternate, more positive thoughts, by becoming better able to adapt to your thought processes, or by allowing yourself to be exposed to the things that scare you.

Compassionate Behavior

With a foundation of compassionate attention and compassionate thinking, you're free to engage in compassionate behavior that embodies your awareness of suffering and your desire to alleviate suffering. Such compassionate behavior allows you to bear your anxiety with warmth and self-kindness, as you move toward living your life fully, with purpose and vitality. Compassion is about being nice to yourself, not in an indulgent way but in a "moving forward" way. If you're agoraphobic, you might find that you're more comfortable sitting at home, but that may be far from compassionate behavior toward yourself. Compassionate behavior in this case means finding the courage to make a commitment to engage with and overcome your anxiety by going out.

Compassionate behavior helps us face up to possible feelings of shame when we seek help for anxiety or depression. Keep in mind, this book is not an alternative to therapy, and if you're feeling depressed or overwhelmed by your anxiety I'd encourage you to seek professional help. Compassionate behavior is very much about opening ourselves to others and allowing our-selves to be helped. Compassionate behavior *is not* about struggling on alone when help is available. Although later I talk about bearing anxiety and living with it in the present moment, compassionate behavior is not about masochistically tolerating pain. Whatever steps you take, do it in the spirit of helpfulness to yourself, with the aim of *developing* yourself *step by step* and getting what help you need as you go.

Compassionate behavior involves self-care, such as establishing regular patterns of sleeping and waking, maintaining a healthy and nourishing diet, and engaging in regular exercise or activities that promote health and release of tension. Sometimes, though, compassionate behavior may involve something we don't typically associate with compassion. For example, gath-ering up the courage to attend an anxiety-provoking meeting because it's important for your professional development may be a form of compassionate behavior. Compassionate behavior may repeatedly involve acts of courage and resolve. For example, a father who's anxious about his teenage daugh-ter's problems with drugs and alcohol may need to summon the courage to compassionately confront her and aim to organize treatment for her prob-lems. When we engage in compassionate behavior, we're consciously taking care of ourselves, even though it may seem distressing at the time. When we cultivate the compassionate mind, we're activating and developing an ancient social mentality that has been designed by evolution to allow us to feel strong and calm, even when we're in the midst of anxiety and a sense of danger.

Other Compassionate Skills

Our circle diagram includes a few other skills that combine with atten-tion, thinking, and behavior to round out the capacities involved in compas-sionate mind training: compassionate *sensory processing* involves being aware of physical sensations in a nonjudgmental, open, and self-compassionate way. This involves learning how to breathe regularly and smoothly (you'll learn about this in part II) and to hold the body in ways that allow you to engage with your anxiety using willingness, mindfulness, and self-kindness. Elements of compassionate sensory processing will be used for some of our imagery-based exercises. As you'll discover, connecting specific sensory expe-riences to your experience of the compassionate mind, such as feeling your facial muscles forming a warm, gently smiling expression, can be helpful in activating your compassion and mindfulness and soothing your anxiety. Compassionate *imagery* involves creating mental images that will stimulate the affiliative, supportive system that fuels and sustains the compassionate mind. If, for example, you allow your mind to brew up a stream of disturbing, frightening images and allow yourself to be so immersed in such images that they begin to dominate your behavior, you run the risk of handing your life over to the domination of your threat-detection system and your threatened mind. If, on the other hand, you deliberately practice focusing on images of compassionate and nurturing figures who accept you and provide you with a safe and soothing place or on images of being compassionate to yourself, you may be able to activate your compassionate mind and begin to manage your anxiety. Developing the skill of compassionate imagery can take some time, and it can be challenging; however, steady, gradual work in this area may begin to offer you new ways of engaging with, and freeing yourself from, excessive experiences of anxiety.

A lot of these skills might seem like things you already use: in our everyday lives we're often moved to help others, to be supportive and kind. The "skillfulness" we're seeking to cultivate in compassionate mind training involves bringing these qualities to life in ourselves and in response to the suffering we encounter in ourselves over the course of our lives. The aim is for us to activate the compassionate mind as we need it, moment by moment, in response to the challenges of life.

The Importance of the Intention to Be Compassionate

The cultivation and generation of feelings of warmth and kindness is an important element of all these attributes and skills. This is where some people begin to struggle. They may say they can feel kindness for others but they can't feel kindness for themselves. This is common; it's only natural to struggle to feel warmly toward ourselves when we're distressed. Thus you might have to wait a bit for the feelings to get going, but the best way to proceed is to nonetheless practice compassionate attention, thinking, and behavior and allow the feelings to follow with time. In other words, it's important to *try* to be warm, kind, and compassionate even when you're "not feeling it." If the appropriate feelings are hard to muster at first, they'll come later, with practice. If you were in a bad mood, wouldn't you try to be kind to your family, even if you didn't feel like it? Aren't you a member of your family?

As you begin to function in more compassionate ways, perhaps even to extend your heart and hands toward others, your mind will become more sensitive to both your own and others' emotions. You may become better able to notice and discern the quality of your own anxiety and the anxiety of those around you, without this anxiety feeling as if it may be a catastrophe in and of itself. When you're intimately in contact with your own experience, moment by moment, you may be willing to experience life just as it presents itself, which may include the experience of anxious feelings and thoughts.

PART II

Compassionate Mind Training for Anxiety

6

Mindfulness as a Foundation for Compassionate Attention

The brain can only assume its proper behaviour when consciousness
is doing what it is designed for: not writhing and whirling to get out
of present experience, but being effortlessly aware of it.

—Alan Watts, *The Wisdom of Insecurity*[1]

As I said earlier, given that you're holding this book, you probably have some experience with anxiety. Having read this far, you also may have begun to understand something about self-compassion and the motivation to overcome problems with anxiety. I'm glad that you've let yourself take the time to explore how our evolutionary origins have led us to possess a capacity for self-compassion that can help us to experience calmness, flexibility, and courage, even in the presence of anxiety. You now can capitalize on what you've learned so far and begin to directly engage in compassionate mind training, using the techniques of CFT.

MINDFULNESS

Jon Kabat-Zinn famously defined mindfulness as the kind of awareness that emerges from paying attention in a particular way: on purpose, in the present moment, and nonjudgmentally.[2] It's one of those things better understood through experience than by explanation: imagine how much more you could learn about swimming by being in the water than by reading about the backstroke. You can easily experience mindfulness by practicing some fundamental exercises that work with your attention, moment by moment. We'll get to some of these shortly; however, mindful awareness is far more than a practiced method of meditation, and the aim is for it to become a way of being that allows you to encounter each experience with a growing degree of openness, acceptance, and self-compassion.

Over the past several years, mindfulness training has become an increasingly popular and important part of Western therapy, and a great deal of the emphasis on the benefits of mindfulness training has involved helping people deal with anxiety-related stress, which is, as we discussed earlier, linked to the activation of our threatened minds. So, it makes sense that we begin with mindfulness when we begin to train ourselves to develop our compassionate response to anxiety.

For just a moment, let's look a little bit more closely at the origins of practicing mindfulness. While much traditional wisdom uses attention-training exercises that resemble what we call mindfulness, the CFT concept of mindfulness is derived from the methods of the Buddha. The Sanskrit term that is now translated into English as "mindfulness" was "*sati,*" which describes a particular, deliberate way of paying attention that involves a blend of present-moment-focused attention, open awareness, and memory of oneself.[3] *Sati* wasn't pursued as an end unto itself but was used as a way of deliberately opening and shifting awareness to promote healthier and more "wholesome" states of mind, such as the state of being compassionate and wise.[4] According to the Buddha, training in *sati* was important for overcoming anxious and apprehensive states of mind.

DIRECTLY LEARNING ABOUT ATTENTION

So far, you've learned a few things about mindfulness by reading. However, learning to be mindful is ultimately an *experiential* process: in other words, the only way to really learn mindfulness is by doing it. So, here's an attention-training exercise that will prepare the way for your mindfulness practice.

Attention Exercise 1

This first exercise can be viewed as a game or experiment that can teach us about the nature of attention. It doesn't take a great deal of time or a whole lot of effort.

1. Sit quietly for a moment and concentrate on your left foot. Notice the feeling in your toes and in the sole of the foot.

2. After about twenty seconds, switch your concentration to your right foot, noticing the sensations present in your heel, your toes, and so on.

3. About twenty seconds later, bring your attention to your fingers by gently rubbing your thumbs over your fingertips.

4. Take a moment, and then with your next natural exhale let this exercise go.

   What happened to your awareness of your fingers when you were focusing on your left foot? What happened to your awareness of your right foot when you were focusing on your fingers?

You've just noticed that, as you redirect your attention, what you're paying attention to takes up more of your mind than what you were previously paying attention to; what you were previously paying attention to fades from your consciousness.

Attention, then, helps to focus awareness; it acts like a sort of zoom lens that brings into focus one particular thing at a time.

Attention Exercise 2

Sit quietly for a minute and simply remember a time when you were happy, when somebody made you really laugh, when you heard a funny joke, or when you were outside enjoying the sunshine on a beautiful spring day. Remember it in as much detail as you can. How did you feel? Who was with you? Notice what happens to your feelings as you focus your attention on this memory; notice how you may even want to smile again.

Okay, now take a breath and bring something new to mind: for just a few moments recall a time when you were upset. Recall what was happening around you, but don't stay in that memory for too long. Notice what happened in your body and what happened to those happy feelings.

Did you feel differently when your attention was directed toward something new?

The changes in your feelings highlight the idea that what we pay attention to influences how we feel and that you can learn to take notice of, and direct the focus of your attention to, *yourself*.

This brief exercise has demonstrated that attention can, to some degree, be *moved around voluntarily*. Though our attention rarely stays put, if we remember our aim, we can return our attention again and again toward a certain orientation.

The exercise has also made you aware of the way the direction of our attention affects the way we feel both physically and mentally, and it's useful to understand this when you begin to deal with your anxiety. In the next few exercises you'll work with your attention and start to connect your attention to the fundamentals of mindfulness.

For the first of these exercises, you'll focus on the natural rhythm of your breathing, allowing your breath to find its own pace and calming rhythm.

Soothing-Rhythm Breathing[5]

Find a comfortable place to sit where you can keep both feet on the floor and can allow your back to be straight. Your spine should not be rigid, but be supple and straight, in a posture described by CFT practitioners as "dignified" or "grounded." Allow your feet to rest approximately shoulder-width apart, and allow your arms to be relaxed and hanging gently, with your hands resting lightly on the tops of your thighs. Make any small adjustments to your posture that you need to be comfortable, and feel free to make such adjustments later if you need. As much as you can, allow yourself to fall silent and still, but allow yourself to feel comfortable and settled rather than trying to rigidly hold on to any particular posture. Now, allow your eyes to close, and draw your attention to the gentle flow of your breath into and out of your body. Feel your connection to your breath as it moves within you and when it is released. Continue to focus on your breath without aiming to change or correct anything at all; simply breathe in…and out.

After a moment, direct your attention to the flow of your breath, feeling it fill your belly as if there were a balloon in your abdomen that gently expands with air as you inhale and then collapses as you exhale. Feel your diaphragm move down and your ribcage grow rounder as you inhale, then feel your diaphragm relax and your ribcage contract as you exhale.

Notice next the movement of your belly as it expands and contracts, yet all the while allow your breath to find its own rhythm and its own pace. You may notice your breathing slightly speed up or slow down. If so, experiment with this for a moment, and ultimately allow the breath to be where it is and how it wishes to be. In this way, your breath is giving way to its own soothing rhythm, moment by moment. With each inhale, connect with the sensation of breathing in; with each exhale, connect with the sensation of breathing out. Allow your breathing to gradually slow down, and with each natural exhale draw your attention to the sensation of letting go with the whole body.

Most often, our breathing becomes somewhat slower and steadier during this practice. It may be helpful to feel the in-breath for a count of three seconds, hold for a moment, and then release the out-breath for a count of three seconds. Taking special care, notice the fullness of the experience of the out-breath.

For a little while, remain attendant to the soothing rhythm of your breath: feel each breath move in, notice the rising and falling of your abdomen, and sense the release of the exhalation. With part of your attention on the flow of your breath, bring some attention now to your feet on the floor, to your legs on the chair, to your back feeling straight and supported, and to the top of your head. Notice the sensation of being grounded and supported in your posture and, through your feet, being connected and rooted to the earth. All the while, the soothing rhythm of your breathing continues, as you follow it with gentle, supportive attention.

During this practice, inevitably your mind will wander. This is perfectly okay and, indeed, a necessary part of your practice. Take a moment to kindly give yourself some credit for noticing that your mind has wandered, and gently return your attention to the breath with the next inhalation. This process of gently noticing where the mind is in the present moment and then gently returning awareness to the breath through the inhalation is at the heart of cultivating mindfulness through soothing-rhythm breathing. No matter how often your mind may wander, simply notice wherever it has gone, then draw your attention back into your body with the next natural inhale. When you notice that your mind has wandered, you're noticing the very nature of the mind and observing that it moves in waves. It's the nature of the mind to wander, and it's the nature of mindfulness practice to gently and nonjudgmentally guide our attention back to the flow of our breath.

After a short while practicing this soothing-rhythm breathing, allow yourself to exhale and let go of the exercise entirely. Before you open your eyes, give yourself some credit for having engaged with this exercise, and recognize that you've taken some very important time to devote attention solely to yourself, as part of a process of cultivating well-being. When you're ready, open your eyes and return to your everyday awareness.

REFLECTING ON YOUR FIRST MINDFULNESS PRACTICE

If you were to begin learning mindfulness exercises with a therapist or meditation instructor, you might follow your first experience of soothing-rhythm breathing with a conversation. With your teacher's guidance, you'd have the opportunity to take the time to reflect and share some of your observations. Since you're learning these practices from this book and may be working on your own, it will be helpful for you to ask these questions of yourself and for yourself. To encourage you to make some space for your experience, and to notice any observations that may be presenting themselves to you, a number of questions are listed below. Please take a few moments to look at these questions and to respond. When you're done, take some time to review your observations.

As we move forward, and as you begin to practice mindfulness, it's a good idea for you to record your observations.

1. What did you notice about your thoughts, feelings, and physical sensations as you engaged in this exercise?

2. How was the attention you experienced during the soothing-rhythm breathing different from your everyday, typical way of paying attention?

3. How might soothing-rhythm breathing help you deal with your anxiety?

4. Were there any obstacles or difficulties that presented themselves as you practiced the soothing-rhythm breathing exercise?

5. How might you bring some of the quality of mindfulness that you experienced in this first exercise to an everyday activity, such as washing dishes or making a cup of tea?

HOW TO PRACTICE

Mindfulness is a quality of attention that requires regular practice; for example, if I hired a personal trainer and went to the gym for one session, this probably wouldn't change the way I look, would it? Likewise, if I planted a sapling it wouldn't become a shady tree overnight. Lots of things take time to grow, and mindfulness is one of them. But evidence shows that, if practiced regularly, mindfulness meditation can significantly reduce anxiety, improve immune function, and change brain activity in as little as eight weeks.[6] Beyond mindfulness, training to cultivate your compassionate mind will involve some form of regular practice, and it's a good idea to begin by committing to setting aside a small amount of time each day for this purpose. It may vary from week to week, but commitment of some time and some consistency of effort will be of great benefit.

Typically, it's a good idea to begin to practice mindfulness daily for at least the first few weeks. This would serve as a good foundation for building your compassionate attention. I know that it might seem daunting at first, but beginning in this way is an act of self-kindness and self-compassion that can have gradual but profoundly positive effects on your anxiety. Regardless, it's important to start where you are and practice however you can. Some of the exercises ahead can take as little as three minutes, and when you become more practiced you'll find that you're able to bring compassionate and mindful attention to your state of being in the space of a single breath. Our work in CFT involves a gradual, gentle approach to the cultivation of capacity for mindful self-compassion, so it's useful to think about what you can aim for and to observe your experience moment by moment, day by day, and week by week as you continue to practice.

As you encounter the exercises in this book, read through the instructions before you begin, then recall the central ideas and steps as you engage in the practice on your own. People often find it helpful to begin mindfulness training with an audio guide. If you wish, you can download audio examples of similar exercises from my website, mindfulcompassion.com, and listen to them on your computer or MP3 player.

WHERE TO PRACTICE

It'd be a good idea to establish a regular setting to which you can return repeatedly to easily enter into and begin each exercise. This may be a quiet place in your home, or even in your office, where you're likely not to be interrupted. It doesn't have to be anywhere special, spiritual, or religious, but it does help if it's somewhere that feels safe and a space that you can devote solely to yourself, with a compassionate intention for your own well-being.

For a number of exercises, you'll be sitting with your back straight and supported for a period of several minutes, and it'd be good if you could find a comfortable chair, or even a cushion designed for meditation. It might also be helpful to devote some care to how your space looks and feels. Many people who regularly practice mindfulness and compassionate mind training will pay close attention to the cleanliness and the beauty of the space they devote to meditation and practice. When such a space is free from clutter and feels organized, it can be a mirror to the clarity that we seek. Sometimes, people find it helpful to display images or personal items that embody compassion or that they find pleasant. These can be symbolic items, such as a picture that has special meaning or a beautiful feather you found when you were on a walk. People who meditate under spiritual traditions, such as Buddhism, Hinduism, or Christianity, may choose symbols from their faiths that remind them of ideas like forgiveness, acceptance, or loving-kindness; however, despite drawing on some Buddhist ideas, the practice this book describes requires nothing with any spiritual association.

Overall, the aim is to allow yourself to take just a little time to set aside a space that feels like the right environment for you to pursue a greater sense of well-being, contentment, and calm.

As you cultivate compassionate attention, you may encounter some anxiety-provoking experiences, and some people find that the safe environment they've created for their mindful meditation can help them feel safe and supported.

WHEN TO PRACTICE

It might not be surprising that many of us find it difficult to squeeze even a fifteen-minute mindfulness exercise into our heavily scheduled, demanding days. Many of the clients I've worked with over the years have found it challenging to develop a consistent mindfulness practice because "it's so hard to find the time." In my experience, finding the time to develop a mindfulness practice can be particularly challenging for people who experience high levels of anxiety and often worry that if they set aside some time for the development of their own mindfulness and self-care, they'll be overlooking something else very important. All too frequently, people who are struggling with feelings of shame and anxiety, and who are striving to prove that they are "good enough," find it challenging to set aside time for themselves. Remember, though, that making the decision to cultivate mindfulness and learning to begin to move toward the development of the compassionate mind is, in itself, an act of self-compassion. It can give us a place to rest in the present moment and activate our experience of a secure, safe, and stable relationship with ourselves.

Establishing a regular time for practice—and, as much as possible, returning to the practice with reliability and consistency—can be important to personal growth, and it can be rewarding. Beginning your day with mindfulness practice can set the tone for the rest of the day by turning your mind and attention toward a nonjudgmental, open, and receptive experience of the present moment. For this reason, I often recommend that mindfulness be scheduled as a part of your morning routine. However, although mindfulness training is particularly well suited for a morning practice, it's more important that you establish regularity and find a time of day that will work best for you. It's more important to have consistent practice than to schedule your practice at a particular time of day that may not suit you. Generally speaking, even five minutes of formal mindfulness training on a daily basis will be more beneficial than longer periods of irregular practice.

Recording your daily practice—recording the times when you've engaged in mindfulness training and whatever observations you might have—can really support and sustain your work. The form below can help you follow your progress, structure your work, and reflect on what you've learned, day by day and week by week. You can use this form for any of the mindfulness practices that follow.

Weekly Mindfulness Practice Record

	Length of time in practice, if any:	Did you use an audio guide? (Yes or No)	What did you notice?
Monday Date:			
Tuesday Date:			
Wednesday Date:			
Thursday Date:			
Friday Date:			
Saturday Date:			
Sunday Date:			

FURTHER MINDFULNESS EXERCISES

In CFT, mindfulness training typically begins with soothing-rhythm breathing, but there are a range of other mindfulness practices that can prepare you to access and activate self-compassion in response to anxiety, worry, and fear. The following exercises may be used regularly to cultivate mindful awareness. I recommend that you choose one exercise for a given one- to three-week period to give yourself the chance to explore and deepen your practice of this exercise before moving on to another.

When anxiety arrives, we notice it in our thoughts, our emotional reactions, and also our physical sensations; however, by bringing mindful awareness to the body, we can change our relationship to our anxious physical sensations and respond with greater flexibility and temper the activation of our threat-detection system.

The Body Scan is an exercise that many people find particularly effective for calmly and restfully dealing with stress, and it's well suited to teach us to work with anxiety using our attention. It helps us direct a mindful, nonjudgmental awareness of the body at a gradual and deliberate pace.

The Body Scan[7]

The exercise is usually conducted lying down, or seated with the back straight yet supple. It's best if you find a comfortable space and use a yoga mat, rug, or blanket to lie on. The temperature should also be comfortable. Choose a time for this exercise when you'll be free from distraction or interruption for at least fifteen and up to forty-five minutes.

To begin, let your eyes close, and allow yourself to rest but not sleep. Allow yourself to fall silent and still. Gently direct your attention to the physical sensations you're experiencing, and bring your attention to the presence of life in the body.

Allow yourself to observe the flow of your breath as it moves gently into and out of your body. There's no need to breathe in any special way; just allow the breath to find its own rhythm. As you breathe in, notice the physical sensations involved in the inhalation. When you release the breath, allow your attention to flow out with the exhalation.

With each in-breath, gather and collect attention; with each out-breath, let go of that awareness.

Now, gently direct your attention to the physical sensations you're experiencing throughout your body at this moment. With each inhalation, allow your attention to gather at the points where your body meets the mat, the chair, or the cushion that supports you, and feel your weight sinking into them. As you exhale, notice the heaviness you feel as your weight seems to sink further.

Note: There's no need to aim for any special state of being during this practice. There's no need to strive to relax or to do anything but simply observe what you're experiencing moment by moment. Let go of the urge to judge, analyze, or even describe your experience, then begin to direct your attention to the different parts of your body.

With the next natural inhale, allow your attention to move to the physical sensations in your abdomen. Notice the various sensations that accompany each in-breath and out-breath. After staying with this experience for a few seconds, bring your attention up from your abdomen, along the length of your left arm, and into your left hand. Allow your attention to spread, as if it were a warm presence radiating down your arm, all the while noticing the presence of life in your body.

Merely observe the sensations in your hand. With each inhale, allow yourself to imagine the breath flowing into your chest and abdomen and radiating down your left arm into your hand. Your attention will accompany this inhalation, as if you were inhaling awareness of the physical sensations present in your hand. Allow yourself to breathe in to the sensations in each part of your hand for several seconds. With each exhale, allow yourself to let go of that awareness.

As you do this, allow yourself to notice your thumb…index finger…second finger…ring finger…and pinky. Next, breathe in a collected awareness of the sensations in the back of your hand…the palm of your hand…and your hand as a whole. When you feel that you've completed your gentle observation of the sensations in your left hand, allow your attention to radiate back up your left arm, noticing the presence of life in your lower arm, your biceps, your triceps, and all of the parts of your arm.

With the next natural inhale, allow your attention to gather again in your abdomen. Next, allow yourself to bring this attention to the sensations in your right arm and hand, in the same manner that you used with your left.

At a comfortable pace, and with an attitude of gentle, nonjudgmental curiosity, direct your attention to each of the areas of your body in turn. Take your time and spend as long as you need, before exhaling and letting go of this area and moving the attention to the next part of your body. Breathe in to the sensations in each foot (and each of the toes)…each lower leg…shin…and calf… pelvic region…lower back and abdomen…upper back and shoulders…neck…

and the contact point between your head and your spine, just behind your eyes...Now, bring attention to the muscles of your face...forehead...and scalp.

Allow yourself to take this slowly, and when you observe discomfort or tension in any part of your body, allow yourself to again breathe in to the sensations. As much as you can, attempt to stay with each sensation, merely observing it, being with it moment by moment. Remember that it's the nature of our minds to wander. When you notice that your mind has drifted away from the focus on physical sensations, accept that this has happened, allow some room for this experience in your awareness, and gently draw your attention back to your physical sensations with the next natural inhale.

After you've spent some time engaged in this practice, having brought a mindful awareness to your body over the course of several minutes, gently allow your breath and attention to return to settle on the physical sensations in the abdomen.

Now, with the next natural inhale, allow your attention to focus on the sounds that surround you in the room, then to the sounds outside the room. Following this, allow your attention to gently settle on the sounds even farther away than that. Giving yourself a few moments to gather your attention and orientation to your presence in the room, you can open your eyes and resume your daily activities.

The Body Scan is a useful practice to engage in regularly for a period of at least two weeks, in order to begin to experience the effect of regular, mindful release of tension and the direction of flexible, focused, and non-judgmental attention to your experience of stress and anxiety in the body. You can use the log in the previous section to record your practice of the Body Scan.

The next exercise, Soften, Soothe, and Allow, is one that many of my patients have benefited from as a daily practice. It helps us see how we can use mindfulness to make space for our experience of anxiety and helps us see how we might apply mindful and compassionate attention to our experience of distress.

Soften, Soothe, and Allow[8]

Just as with the other mindfulness and compassionate-attention exercises, begin by adopting a stable and grounded posture, with your back straight and supported. Settle upon your cushion or chair and allow your breathing to settle into the natural pace and rhythm that emerges through your soothing-rhythm breathing. When you're ready, take three more breaths in this way, feeling the release of tension each time you exhale.

With the next natural inhale, direct part of your attention to the sensations present in your body. Whatever you notice, allow yourself to continue to focus also on your breath, feeling the movement of your belly, and bring open, non-judgmental attention to the presence of your breath in the area of your heart.

With each inhale, bring compassionate attention into your body; with each exhale, let go of tension. Pay attention to any experience of emotions in your body. What physical sensations, in this moment, feel related to your emotions? Perhaps you've experienced anxiety or distress; if so, this is the time to allow yourself to feel where this emotional experience presents itself as a physical sensation. You may feel anxiety as tension in your chest or throat, for example. Wherever it is, notice it, and bring compassionate attention to this place with each inhale, and feel yourself softening into that space in your body. Imagine this as similar to applying heat to relieve stiff or sore muscles. Let go of physically forcing anything at all, and repeat the word "soft" over and over again, with the soothing rhythm of the breath. There's no aim to suppress or avoid any experience at all here; you're simply bringing mindful and compassionate attention to your emotional and physical experience in this very moment. Stay with this process of softening for a few minutes.

Having softened into this experience, now, if you like, bring one of your hands to your chest, just over your heart. Feel the warmth of your hand, and through it direct kindness and soothing thoughts to yourself. Recognize your struggle, and direct warmth and acceptance toward yourself and your experience. Speak kindly to yourself, out loud or in your thoughts, validating your struggle with anxiety and distress and connecting with your compassionate inner voice—for example: *I can see how hard this has been for me now. This pain and these difficult experiences are a part of life, and this is not my fault. May I grow into greater well-being, peacefulness, and happiness, moment by moment.*

Next, gently repeat the word "soothe" in your mind, with part of your attention resting in the soothing rhythm of your breath. You may also choose to imagine the experience of soothing and kindness arriving at that place in your body where you've felt your emotion physically affect you. Notice your inhale and exhale as much as you can. Remain with this process of soothing for a few more minutes.

As a final step, consciously let go of the need or urge to get rid of your emotional experience. As you exhale, let go of any effort to avoid or suppress your emotion. Having softened into the experience, and having brought soothing attention to your struggle, ask yourself to allow your discomfort to be just as it is in this moment. The feeling doesn't need to be pushed away. You're in a safe place, and you can just allow this emotion to be where it is for now and to go in its own time. This time, silently repeat the word "allow" in time with the soothing rhythm of your breath. Just as you have at each step of this practice, stay with this for a few minutes, or for however long feels right to you.

You may choose to silently repeat the words "soften, soothe, allow" in your mind as you follow your breath during the last minutes of the exercise. Stay with your breath for as long as you need, resting in the soothing rhythm and directing mindful, compassionate attention to your emotion.

When you're ready, take one last inhale, then exhale slowly and let go of this exercise altogether, giving yourself credit for having deeply engaged with this practice.

Like the earlier mindfulness exercises, Soften, Soothe, and Allow can be used daily for a period of several days, weeks, or months. This practice, however, may also be used in an abbreviated form to bring compassionate attention into contact with anxiety in the moment it appears to you, wherever you are. This will represent an important transition point, where your practice of mindful awareness begins to move from the meditation cushion to your day-to-day emotion-regulation responses. The Three-Minute Breathing Space and Mindful Walking will take this application of mindfulness skills further into the flow of your everyday life.

The Three-Minute Breathing Space[9]

As the name implies, this exercise involves only a small time investment, but it can bring enormous benefits and help you become calm when you begin to suffer from anxiety.

Sit with the soles of your feet touching the ground and your back upright yet supported and comfortable, in a dignified and erect yet relaxed manner. Feel yourself rooted to the earth at the points where your body meets your chair and the floor. Allow your eyes to close or, if you prefer, just allow your eyelids to relax as you cast your gaze gently at the floor. Now, direct part of your attention to the soles of your feet and then to the flow of experience that unfolds in your mind. Observing thoughts, feelings, and physical sensations, allow yourself to notice, as much as you can, what presents itself to you at this moment, paying particular attention to those feelings, ideas, and sensations that may be unpleasant or upsetting. Rather than pushing these away, allow them to be just as they are. Take a moment to allow yourself to simply acknowledge the presence of these experiences, making space for whatever emerges and flows through your field of inner observation.

Now, having allowed yourself to sit in the presence of this moment, with whatever it brings, change your focus and direct your attention toward your breath. Observe your breathing, and direct your attention to the movements of your body as you exhale and inhale. Take special notice of the bellows-like movement of your abdomen, as your body gently allows the air to move in and out, moment by moment. Take a minute to stay with the flow of your breath and allow your attention to blend with the movement of breathing itself, as best as you can.

Next, allow the scope of your awareness to widen to gradually encompass your entire body. As you inhale, bring your attention into your body as a whole and sense your body gently expanding; as you exhale, completely let go of that awareness. Stay with this experience for about a minute, and allow yourself to make space within your body and mind, as best as you can, for whatever arrives.

Next, begin to let go of this exercise, by directing part of your attention again to the soles of your feet, then to the top of your head, then to everything in between. When you're ready, allow your eyes to open, and let go of this exercise entirely.

If possible, make time to practice the Three-Minute Breathing Space several times a day, in addition to a daily, regular mindfulness practice, such as Soften, Soothe, and Allow or the Body Scan. At first, practice the Three-Minute Breathing Space while seated; later, try to engage with the exercise while standing. This brief exercise can also be used as a coping response during those moments when you feel the intensification of stress and anxiety.

Mindfulness is more than just a technique for addressing problems, however. It's a natural, human state of being that can allow us to more fully experience the richness of the present moment. As such, you should aim to gradually bring this state of mindful acceptance into other areas of your life so you can learn to take mindful action. A good place to begin this transition is with the simple act of walking. The following exercise will teach you how to begin to integrate mindfulness into all of your activities.

Mindful Walking[10]

Find a place, inside or outside, where you may walk for fifteen to twenty minutes with relatively little concern for onlookers or interruptions. You might choose a park, a city block, a shopping mall, or even a path through the rooms of your home. Begin by standing with your feet slightly less than shoulder-width apart. Keep your knees supple, your back straight, and your arms relaxed. Gaze forward but with a wide-angle focus. As you inhale, direct your attention toward the soles of your feet. Allow yourself to sense the connection between your feet and the floor. With each inhale, observe the presence of life in your legs and feet, feeling the distribution of your weight throughout your body; then, with each exhale, let go of this awareness. After some time experiencing this, slowly transfer your weight to your right leg, taking note of all of the richness of the sensations involved. Next, allow your attention to focus on your left leg and transfer your weight to it. You may experience a sensation of the right leg feeling lighter or "emptying" as you rely on it less for support. Allow your attention now to be divided between your legs, noticing the different sensations present throughout your lower body.

When you're ready, allow your left foot to slightly lift away from the floor. Notice the sensations in your muscles as it lifts and then gently moves forward to take a first step. Gradually and deliberately move your left leg forward, all the while gently observing the physical sensations that accompany this action. As you complete this first step, notice the sensations involved as you place your left foot back on the floor. Feel your weight transfer as your body uses your leg and foot for support and as its contact with the ground grows heavier and more assured. As this occurs, notice whatever sensations emerge in your right leg as it lets go of the weight and support, growing lighter as the movement continues. As your weight is transferred to your left foot in a stable fashion, repeat this process with your right foot. Breathe into the sensation of your right foot leaving the floor. Observe the presence of life in your body as your right foot moves forward to take the next step. Again, notice the physical sensations as your foot makes contact with the ground and you complete this next step. As you do this, allow your motion to flow from one step to the next, rather than complete these steps as discrete, robotic movements. Notice how your intention guides your body, drawing it forward slowly in space and time. Your movements may seem as if they're happening in slow motion. Continue to take steps in this fashion, continuing along the path you've chosen. As you do this, keep some of your attention connected to the flow of your breath and to the spreading sensations throughout your body.

As you walk, connect your attention to the presence of life throughout your body, noticing with kindness and gentle acceptance any sensations that present themselves. Keep your gaze softly focused ahead of you, aware of your surroundings, but also persistently aware of your presence in your body. As with earlier practices, your mind will inevitably wander from the act of walking. Whenever this occurs, take note of where your mind is focused at that moment, and kindly direct your attention back to the act of walking. It may be useful to use the sensation of your feet on the ground or the relaxed straightness of your spine as a focal point to draw your attention back to the physical sensations that emerge moment by moment.

Your pace should now be moderately slow, but reasonably comfortable. In time you may find yourself walking at a more "normal" pace. Note any tendency to speed up excessively, as you'd notice any distraction in your mindfulness practice, and gradually allow yourself to return your attention to the physical sensations of walking, anchoring your awareness through your breath and through your physical contact with the ground.

When you've concluded this practice, allow yourself to exhale fully and completely let go of the exercise, giving yourself credit for having engaged in this work and moving toward developing greater mindfulness and compassion.

After working with this exercise for a few days or weeks, you might choose to bring the same quality of awareness to other activities, making the transition to applied mindful awareness. In this way you might have the experience of connecting with your observing self as you go through your everyday life.

CHALLENGES ON THE PATH TO MINDFULNESS AND COMPASSION

As you engage in mindfulness training, you'll probably come into contact with some obstacles and challenges. This is a normal part of any endeavor. I doubt anyone ever set out to learn to play the violin or the guitar without hitting the wrong notes or having sore fingers. Learning involves stumbling and confusion. A compassionate and mindful awareness of your step-by-step learning can allow you to embrace the process, rather than descend into self-criticism and shame. Cultivating a compassionate mind involves a gradual development of your inborn, intuitive wisdom and requires patience and consistency. Never punish or judge yourself if you feel like you're not making sufficient progress—try to accept yourself as you are in the present moment.

Let's take a look at some of the challenges and potential problems you may face, so that you're ready if you encounter them. The challenges we face in cultivating mindfulness and compassion are often things that we can't work around, but we can work *through* them.

Trouble Letting Go of Judgments

Although you might intellectually grasp the notion of nonjudgmental awareness, you may still stubbornly cling to judgments. This is to be expected and is a part of the ongoing process.

For example, after doing a mindfulness exercise, you might wonder whether you've done it the "right" way; however, for our purposes, as long as you've allowed yourself time to sit with your experience and observe the flow of your attention, you've done the exercise right. Mindfulness is a practice of *being* rather than *doing*, and it really is one of the few human activities that allows us to totally let go of the idea of "getting it right." I find it helpful, particularly on days when my mind seems too active to sit still, to remind myself of the Buddhist saying that "as soon as we sit on the meditation cushion we are already enlightened."

Keep in mind that mindfulness is the nonjudgmental observation of the contents of consciousness, and compassion is the nonjudgmental awareness of the observer herself.

Trouble Staying Awake

Another challenge to practicing the exercises is staying awake! For example, the deep relaxation that results from the Body Scan may lull some of my clients to sleep. This response is completely normal, but it's important to remind yourself that, with practice, the Body Scan becomes more an exercise of "falling awake" than of falling asleep. With practice this will happen naturally, so if you find yourself falling asleep in the beginning, see whether you can open your heart with compassionate self-acceptance and just let yourself be where you are in the process. That's much more in tune with our aims than struggling to "be better." If you have particular difficulty staying awake during mindfulness work, even after several weeks of practice, you may opt to practice with your eyes open, and direct your attention to a space on the floor or an object in the room that you find comforting. Whatever you need to do to adapt these practices to work for you, the key is that you keep engaging and experimenting and practicing.

The aim is for compassionate mind practice to ease your anxiety and to activate your affiliation system—that accepting, soothing system within yourself—to form a secure base from which to operate in the world with compassion and courage.

Trouble Relaxing

Although mindfulness can be relaxing, people often report that they feel anxious or experience difficult emotions during their daily practice. Sometimes this can make it seem as if the mindfulness-training techniques didn't work; but, in fact, bringing mindful awareness into contact with anxiety may be exactly *how* this practice works. During the practice of mindfulness, the aim is to fully experience whatever may unfold before your mind, moment by moment, in a spirit of willingness, curiosity, and openness. This is different from pushing away and avoiding uncomfortable experiences or attempting to control your emotions. By experiencing your anxiety in this new way, you open the door to compassionate attention and prepare yourself to come into greater acceptance of who you are and rest in the presence of your compassionate mind. You may actively learn that attempts to control and suppress anxious emotional experiences may actually be amplifying and perpetuating your distress. Mindful acceptance and compassionate attention directed toward yourself can help you break this cycle and help you cope with your experiences.

The Five Hindrances

Traditional Buddhist writings on mindfulness and liberation from anxious suffering describe five potential roadblocks to cultivating mindfulness. These obstacles are sometimes known as the Five Hindrances.[11] Let's take a look at these natural human tendencies and try to find ways to open the door for compassion.

The first of these hindrances involves a craving for pleasurable experiences. The pull of something appealing in your environment or even in your imagination can persistently draw you to be hooked by the craving for and fixation with desirable or exciting thoughts, images, and experiences. This natural tendency can distract you during mindfulness training, but when you notice these distractions and preoccupations, you simply need to make space for them, acknowledge them, and bring your attention back to the present moment with your next inhalation. You may need to repeat this several times, but each time knowing that you're practicing a new way of relating to an experience that can dominate your thoughts, images, and feelings and, as a result, your behavior. You're also practicing the ability to observe and balance your emotion-regulation system, allowing for the eventual activation of your compassionate affiliation system.

The second of these classical Buddhist hindrances is ill will, which refers to a preoccupation with memories of painful emotions, a preoccupation with emotional and physical pain (or discomfort) in the present moment, or concern about pain in the future. This can be anything from a persistent itch or cramp to a nagging memory of a lost opportunity. Habitual entanglement with painful experiences, irritants, mild discomfort or itching, or anything generally unpleasant can be a persistent and challenging distraction, but you can meet these distractions with mindful acceptance and, after exhaling, return to the present moment.

In these first two hindrances, we can see how attachment to having what we want and getting rid of what we don't want both conspire to redirect and distract us from engagement with the present moment. Through the development of mindfulness and compassionate attention, you can work with these two hindrances by anticipating the pull of sensory experiences, recognizing that this is a natural part of being human and not your fault. Reflecting on your practice, you can recognize that both pleasant and unpleasant inner experiences might arise during mindfulness training and that both can be met with flexible, focused, nonjudgmental attention and by, again and again, returning your attention to the simple, open observation of each individual moment.

The third hindrance to meditation practice is anxiety and restlessness. We can see, in this hindrance, the activation of our threat-detection system, and the ways our always-on, "better safe than sorry" problem-solving machine can get ahold of our whole being, narrow our attention, and shift us away from the directions of our valued aims. The activity of your threat-detection system may result in the urge to fidget while you try to keep your body still during mindfulness practice. Mindfulness training gives us the opportunity to notice and to take action to change these habitual patterns. Through mindfulness, we can practice staying in the presence of anxious agitation, remain open and aware, and bring compassionate attention to our experience throughout the process. This is the first step in conscious activation of our compassionate emotion-regulation system.

The fourth hindrance is known as sloth or torpor; it refers to low energy levels, a state of exhaustion, and a general slowness to respond. This hindrance may manifest itself as "lazy" avoidance, as procrastination, or as the symptoms of low energy and exhaustion that can so often accompany depression or the feeling of being overworked. If you encounter this problem occasionally during your mindfulness practice, you might simply be tired or possibly have overeaten. However, it may also be the result of a strong aversion to fully experiencing some unprocessed emotions that might show up during the practice. Scheduling and commitment to practice even in the face of an urge to procrastinate can be very helpful in overcoming this problem. Working with a teacher or therapist or sharing these experiences with others who are practicing mindfulness training can help you work through these problems. In my own experience, I often have thought, *I'm too tired to practice mindfulness* or *I don't have the energy to sit*. When I hold myself, gently, to the commitment that I have made, and practice mindfulness for even a few minutes, I often find that I have much more energy, and a much greater sense of ease, after sitting. There is no guarantee this will always be the case, but I do find it an encouraging experience, and it helps me return to my practice when my mind is telling me to just avoid it.

The fifth and final hindrance is described as doubt or indecision, which means that it's challenging for us to commit and have clarity of purpose in our practice. When you aren't sure of the outcomes, you may often go back and forth over what to do. Indeed, humans aren't comfortable with ambiguity. We've evolved to treat something that *might* be bad as if it *were* bad. Part of this might be related to a discomfort with uncertainty, which is characteristic of people with chronic worry, known as generalized anxiety disorder. This doubt may also involve self-doubt, arising from a negative belief about your own abilities and strengths. In this, we can see the activation of the blaming and shaming parts of our threat-detection system. Part of mindful-ness training involves the gradual acknowledgment of such doubts as part of the flowing landscape of the mind. So your work lies in applying mindful awareness to whatever arises in this moment; in this way, you won't need to surrender control of your behavior to the stream of emerging private events that continuously presents itself in your mind. This will result in a flow of compassionate attention that will form the foundation for developing your compassionate mind.

Having used mindfulness training as the platform for the development of compassionate attention, we can now proceed to cultivate the capacity for compassionate imagery, compassionate thinking, and compassionate behav-ior through further compassionate mind-training exercises.

7

Compassion-Focused Imagery

When faced with the intensity of your anxiety response, you may often crave relief and escape. As discussed, this is a natural reaction to a perceived threat, as part of the "fight, flight, or freeze" response. Unlike fleeing from dangers in your environment, however, fleeing from anxiety, worry, or panic can amplify and deepen the activation of your threat-detection system. If you're wracked with anxious suffering but escape and avoidance will only make things worse, where are you to go, and what are you to do?

In your work with this book so far, you've begun to explore other ways of addressing your threatened mind. This has led you to a point where you can directly train your mind to activate the capacity for compassion, calm, and courageous acceptance steeped in warmth and inner strength. You're beginning to learn how to direct this capacity to the experience of anxiety. This takes time, and it means that you'll be working directly with your experience of anxiety. This can sound intimidating, yet you're bringing a very powerful ally along with you on this journey: your compassionate, tolerant mind.

THE POWER OF THE IMAGINATION

The skills and attributes of the compassionate mind can help you focus on the present with a sense of strength and stillness, even when things seem to fall apart around you. Your compassionate mind stimulates a part of you that possesses courage and authority when faced with fearful situations. When we use the compassionate mind, we're awakening an evolved capacity to operate effectively while still in the presence of our anxiety. One of the most powerful tools that we have in cultivating the compassionate mind is our capacity for imagery, which can be used to help us activate different emotions and physical sensations. For example, you've seen that what you focus your attention on can affect how you feel. Similarly, when you imagine an event, your whole being can respond as though this mental event had actually happened, and this can create trouble due to anxiety. You might imagine a potential disaster, become fearful, and then avoid the situation you worry about. If you're hungry and imagine a meal, you can stimulate your salivary glands. Similarly, if you imagine scenes of a sexual nature, you may feel aroused. This basic human ability for the imagination to stimulate systems in the brain and body can also be harnessed to stimulate the compassionate mind and, in turn, the soothing system. And, crucially, if we engage with compassionate imagery, then we can activate systems in our brain that will help us tolerate and cope with anxiety.

THE ROOTS OF IMAGERY

Many of my clients say, "I can't do imagery; I'm no good at it." The simple act of guiding the imagination can seem too difficult and, as we know by now, it doesn't take long for us to start judging ourselves if we find something difficult. Nevertheless, I've found that resistance to the use of imagery to build self-compassion is usually driven by a misunderstanding of imagery as needing to be sophisticated or complex. Often, people think they have to create high-definition, three-dimensional pictures or cinema-sized screens in their minds! But it requires no such excellence and no special talent. Imagery, basically, is fleeting, impressionistic, and unique to each person, and it's the emotions and the focus of your attention that are really important during exercises that use your imagination. Say I were to casually ask you what your car looks like, what you had for breakfast, or what kind of summer vacation you'd like. Any consideration of an answer to such a question uses imagery. The images called to mind might not be sharp and may only be fleeting and fragmentary, but that's all you need. The clarity of the image is not important; rather, it's the sensations and feelings that emerge that we're interested in.

Imagery, or visualization, has been used for millennia by different cultures: ancient Hindu priests would visualize the fire within them and feel the warmth of a divine presence; Jewish mystics visualize the presence of God in themselves and in the universe; within the Christian tradition there are many examples of prayers that evoke and involve visualization; in Buddhist contemplative practices there's a long tradition of using specific visualizations to access parts of the self, such as the compassionate self, in order to alleviate suffering. Similarly, CFT uses visualization to help activate and engage our compassionate selves and our affiliative emotion-regulation system so that it's ready to deal with and cope with what matters most to us in our lives. CFT techniques, however, draw on evidence-based psychotherapy methods, the neuroscience of emotions, behavioral theory, and evolutionary science, rather than being based solely on ancient cultural traditions. This allows us to test and explore the hypotheses that have guided and driven spiritual and philosophical practices for centuries and to continue to discover how best to alleviate and come to terms with our struggle with anxiety.

SIX IMAGERY EXERCISES

You can use the following series of exercises as an introduction to compassionate imagery and then adopt them as regular, daily practices in training your compassionate mind. Many of the same principles of structured, consistent practice that you learned in the previous chapter will be helpful, but for now I suggest that you take the time to experience each of these exercises for yourself. If you're working with a therapist or teacher, you might want to discuss your responses to the imagery with them. If you're working on your own, you can document your observations. Recordings of these exercises can be found at mindfulcompassion.com. It's important that you begin to practice these exercises at a pace that feels comfortable. As you become familiar with one series of exercises, feel free to move on to the next series.

In these meditative-like practices, you begin with a gentle focus on the rhythm of your breath, then use your imagination to activate your soothing, compassion-focused emotion-regulation system. The first compassionate-imagery exercise, Creating a Safe Place, has two functions. First, it helps direct your attention toward the sense of feeling safe. The practice of imagining a safe place for yourself allows you to explore and be curious about what kind of things will be important to you to evoke feelings of safety. Sometimes, if you're feeling a bit stressed out, taking time to just imagine a safe place can give you somewhere to rest. Secondly, creating a safe place helps you imagine somewhere that gives you a sense of joy. For example, because this place is your creation and is from your own imagination, it's a place that welcomes you—possibly, as one of my clients described it, as if it's a place where your dog wags its tail and barks happily to welcome you when you return home. But you need to find your own ways of thinking about it. The place you create is meant to embody compassionate warmth and safety. In this exercise, you are allowing yourself to experience feelings of being safe already, of already abiding in a place where you're relaxed and confident about your well-being.

When you feel anxious, a sense of contentment and security may seem miles away; however, the mind responds to the imagination as though what unfolds may be real. We've learned that we've evolved to feel comfort in the presence of strong, supportive attachment figures who can activate this sense of safety, and we know that in this way we have an inborn capacity to use our imagination and cultivate feelings of safety and activate our self-soothing system.

Creating a Safe Place[1]

Begin this exercise as you might begin the soothing-rhythm breathing, by lying comfortably on a mat or sitting in a comfortable, secure posture on a chair or meditation cushion. Take some time to allow a few mindful breaths to move in and out of your body. Now, turn your attention to your imagination and begin to think about a happy, secure place that surrounds you. Perhaps it's a place you've visited, somewhere from your past, or even somewhere you've only thought about visiting. It's important that this place be somewhere calm, such as a shady picnic spot, or a seaside balcony, or a cozy chair by the fireside in winter; whatever it may be, this place is just for you, and you're free to imagine anywhere that feels right to you.

If you imagine a serene, sandy beach, feel the smooth, soft sand beneath your feet and the warmth of the sunlight. Do you hear the waves lapping against the shoreline? Or the seagulls calling?

If you imagine somewhere secure, cozy, and warm, such as a comfortable chair beside the fire, can you feel the heat radiating out to warm you? What do you smell? Can you hear the fire crackling?

You may remember somewhere you've walked among ancient trees and greenery, or somewhere else that holds fond memories for you, when you were supported, loved, and able to experience a sense of playfulness. In order to vividly evoke such images, recall what it was like, or what it may be like if you were actually there, right now. Notice, for example, the quality of the light, the texture of the sand, the fabric of the chair, or the bark of the tree, and notice the sounds, smells, and temperature.

Remain with this visualization for a few minutes, from time to time noting the natural rhythm of your breathing, feeling your belly rising and falling with the even pace of the breath. Whenever your mind wanders, draw your attention back to the image of your safe space with the next natural inhale. After a few minutes, allow the image to fade, and gradually let go of the entire exercise with the next natural exhale, and return your awareness to your actual surroundings.

This next exercise will help you imagine yourself in a very different way than you might be accustomed to, as if you're an actor rehearsing a role in a play or a film. The exercise involves the creation of the personification of your compassionate self, whom you'll meet later.

Building and Becoming the Compassionate Self

Take a moment to imagine what qualities your compassionate self would ideally have. What qualities would help you have a calm, confident, and compassionate presence. Would you be wise? Strong, able to tolerate discomfort? Would you have warm feelings toward others and toward yourself? Would you feel empathy for someone else's suffering and for their behavior? Would you be understanding of others' faults and foibles and as a result nonjudgmental, accepting, kind, and forgiving? Would you have courage? Write these qualities down. Then ask yourself how you'd picture your most compassionate aspect. Perhaps you might imagine yourself older and wiser, or younger and more innocent. This is *your* exercise, and you're free to design and embellish an image of your compassionate self according to your own desire.

Next, find a place where you'll feel safe and may remain uninterrupted for some time. Ideally, this would be a quiet and special place, such as the one you use for your mindfulness practice. Start the exercise as you would your soothing-rhythm breathing. Allow your eyes to close; bring part of your attention to the soles of your feet as they connect with the floor and to your bottom on the chair. Allow your back to be straight and to feel supported. Next, partly direct your attention to the flow of your breath into and out of your body; allow it to find its own rhythm and pace. Feel yourself breathe in and breathe out. Continue this breathing uninterrupted until you've gathered your attention and feel focused on the present moment.

At this point, recall the qualities of your compassionate self that you wrote down, and now *imagine that you already possess* those qualities. Breathe in as you experience yourself making a wise decision; breathe out. Breathe in and imagine yourself courageously confronting your fears; breathe out. Continue through the list and then imagine all these qualities together...and your ability to be compassionate toward yourself...and toward others. Imagine yourself as a completely nonjudgmental person who doesn't condemn yourself or others for their faults or foibles. Allow yourself to bring to mind the sensory details that you'd notice as your compassionate self. What are you wearing? Is your body relaxed and receptive? Does your body language signal openness and kindness? Are you smiling? If not, smile now, and at the same time imagine the warmth you feel when you carefully hold an infant. As you breathe in, bring attention into your body, imagine yourself expanding, and welcome your ability to be wise, warm, and resilient.

For the next few moments, as you breathe in and out, imagine what the tone of your voice would be if you were this compassionate self. How would you behave? What would the expression on your face be? Allow yourself to take pleasure in your capacity to share kindness with, and care for, both those around you and yourself. If your mind wanders, as so often happens, use your next natural inhale to gently bring your attention back to this image of your compassionate self.

The aim in this moment is to connect the image you created in the beginning with the compassionate image of you at your very best. Can you see the two people standing side by side and then merging into one? For the next several minutes, continue to give mindful attention, returning and refocusing when needed, to this compassionate self.

When you feel ready, with your next natural exhale, allow any attachment to this exercise to simply melt away. Breathe in again, and with the next natural exhale allow yourself to become aware again of your surroundings and then recognize and acknowledge the effort you've invested in this exercise. As you let go, return your attention to your surroundings and carry on with your day.

I'd like to take a moment to put your work here in a little bit of histori-cal context. In Buddhist art there are paintings known as "mandalas," which display the Buddha and other mythological beings within a series of circles. These mandalas represent a map of the inner world of a human being and are symbolic of the various aspects of our personalities: our wisdom, our rage, our joy, and even our lust.

A mandalas or other such images can be used as part of a special medi-tation that employs visualization, sound, and certain small gestures to help evoke the various parts of ourselves so that we may come to terms with all aspects of our being from a broader perspective. The idea is that if we focus our thoughts (in terms of mental images), words (mental or verbal phrases with special meanings), and deeds in the form of unique gestures that connect us with a particular experience, we can then later recall certain aspects of our personality that may help us deal with times when we're suffering.

In order to understand the various parts of your personality, and the way they affect your behavior, it may be helpful to separate these various aspects and look at them individually.

Bringing the Compassionate Self into Contact with the Many Parts of You

There are many different parts of who you are: your angry self, your anxious self, your joyful self. Begin to do some soothing-rhythm breathing and then pause for a moment to reflect on this.

Now imagine having an argument with somebody whom you know to be harsh and critical. What does the angry side of your personality think about this situation? How does it feel in your body to feel criticized or attacked? What behavioral urges arrive in this angry part of yourself? And if this angry part of your personality were to seize control of things, what would it do?

Now, bring your attention back to the flow of your breath, and with your next natural exhale let go of this image of your angry self.

With your next natural inhale, focus on your anxious self and how it might deal with the same argument. What does the anxious part of you think? What are your physical sensations? What would this anxious part of your personality do if it seized control of your behavior?

Now, bring your attention back to the flow of your breath, and with your next natural exhale let go of this image of your anxious self.

With your next natural inhale, focus on the interaction between your angry self and your anxious self. Do they like one another? Does your angry self approve of your anxious self and how it behaves? What does your anxious self think about your angry self? Is it frightened of it? Does the anxious part feel protected by your angry self? And does the angry part feel threatened or stifled by the anxious self?

Now, bring your attention back to the flow of your breath, and, again, with your next natural exhale let go of this image of these two parts of your personality.

These two different parts are really just ways we deal with events as they unfold. Often, these different parts can be in conflict with one another and make us feel in conflict with ourselves; however, when we activate and connect with the compassionate self, things can be quite different. At this point in the exercise, rather than focusing on the anxious or angry aspect of your personality, focus on the wise, calm, authoritative, and compassionate part. Pause and rest in the flow of your breath, and spend a few moments focusing on this part of yourself. See yourself from the outside with a gentle smile on your face, and see other people relating to you as someone who is calm, kind, and wise. Once you've got the sense of this aspect of yourself, imagine this compassionate self dealing with that initial argument. What are your thoughts about the argument now? How does that calm, wise, and compassionate self feel? What's this compassionate self doing when it takes control of your behavior? How would this be different from the way your angry or anxious self behaves?

Now, bring your attention back to the flow of your breath, exhale, and let go of this image.

When different emotions flow through us, they affect the way we feel about ourselves by affecting our thoughts, physical sensations, and behavior. We can let them do their own thing, of course, and let our anger or anxiety run the show—it might seem easier to hand over control that way; but in the long run it's not very helpful or self-compassionate to do so. Compassion gives us courage to take control and hand back our behavior to the parts of us that we know will help us lead our lives calmly and with kindness toward ourselves.

This exercise might have given you a glimpse of what can happen when you start to deliberately and willingly focus your attention toward the kind of self likely to be helpful to you.

The chances are that if you suffer from high levels of anxiety, you're very familiar with your anxious self and possibly also your angry self. You may be familiar with how you become angry with yourself for being anxious and how you become anxious when you feel angry, but less familiar with the way your compassionate self deals with the problem of anxious suffering. But this is what these exercises and practices will help you do: discover how your compassionate self deals with, or helps you cope with, your anxiety.

By this point you've done a lot of work to develop an understanding of the nature of anxiety. You've learned where it comes from and how it can take control of your thoughts and behaviors and that it's *not your fault*; that your always-on, "better safe than sorry" threat-detection system is ready to leap in and take control partly because of the way our brains have evolved and partly because of your personal history. These tricky, complicated brains of ours do allow us to negotiate our way in the world, but we're better off when we understand them somewhat. Thankfully, we also have a capacity for cultivating our self-compassion and our mindful attention to our compassionate selves. Learning how to do so—by embodying and manifesting the strength and wisdom of our compassion—we broaden our outlook and open ourselves to new possibilities.

Experiencing Compassion Flowing In

Find a place where you can sit with your back straight and supported, either in a comfortable chair or on a meditation cushion. Much as with any other exercise in mindfulness and compassion, it's good to find a quiet space where you'll be undisturbed for about ten to twenty minutes when you can allow yourself to devote some attention and energy to yourself.

Start by bringing attention to your breathing by observing its .flow and rhythm, and allow the breath to find its own pace. Observe and remain with this flow for a few minutes.

Next, bring part of your attention into your body, and feel the strength and compassion available to you in your posture. Feel your feet on the floor, your bottom connected to your cushion or chair, and your spine straight and supported. Your posture is grounded and dignified and reflects your sense of calm and self-compassion. Allow a gentle smile to form, and with part of your attention staying with the flow of your breath, begin to remember a pleasant day when someone was compassionate and supportive toward you. This person was nonjudgmental, didn't condemn you, was empathic, and cared about you and your happiness. As much as you can, remember the sensory details of this experience. Can you remember what you were wearing? Where were you? Was it hot? Cold? Raining? Was the wind blowing through the trees, or was the radio on in the background?

Now, bring your attention back to the flow of your breath; inhale and exhale, and stay with this image for a while.

In this exercise, you're focusing your attention on your desire to be kind and helpful, by remembering the experience of receiving such help and kindness. Whenever your mind is inevitably distracted and wanders away from this memory, gather your attention with the next natural inhale, make space for whatever's arising, and simply return your attention to your breath and to the image of this compassionate person with your next natural exhale. As you breathe in again, bring your attention to the facial expression of this person from your past. Allow yourself to remember, as much as you can, his body language and movements. What did this person say to you? How did he say it? Pay particular attention to the tone and sound of his voice. Stay with this experience for a little while, breathing in and out. Next, bring your attention to the quality of the emotion this person had for you. How did he feel toward you? How does this make you feel—do you have any physical sensations as a result of your emotion? Take a few minutes to remain in the presence of that emotion. You may feel safe and protected or as if your body is grounded and stronger. However this emotion shows up, see whether you can welcome it, identify it as mindful compassion, and invite yourself to make space for it. This is a time to bring attention to the experience of compassion flowing into you.

Now, bring your attention back to the flow of your breath. Inhale and exhale smoothly, and take a few moments to stay with the way this experience feels.

As much as you can, connect with the emotions of appreciation, gratitude, and happiness that arrived with this person's care. For as long as feels right to you, perhaps a few minutes more, remain in the presence of this memory and this feeling.

When it feels right, let this experience go: with your next natural exhale, allowing the memory and images to fade away. After a few more slow and even breaths, exhale and let go of this entire exercise. Before you open your eyes and resume your day, take a moment to give yourself credit for engaging with your practice of self-compassion, recognizing that you've made a conscious decision to take care of yourself and move toward the alleviation of your suffering from anxiety.

The next exercise will allow you to build on your practice of mindful, compassionate attention and develop your experience of using imagery to activate your affiliative self-compassion system.

Experiencing Compassion Flowing Out

Find a quiet, safe place for this exercise. Sitting on a chair or cushion, adopt a dignified, meditative posture, with the soles of your feet connected to the floor and your back straight and supported. Start by following your breath in and out of your body, and become aware of your physical presence, just as it is, in this very moment. Allow your breath to find its own rhythm and pace. Whenever your attention wanders, you can gently and consistently draw it back to this moment, by focusing again on your breath.

After a few minutes, having gathered and collected your attention in a mindful and compassionate way, bring your attention to a time when you felt compassionate toward another person when this person was in need of a helping hand. You can even bring your attention instead toward the compassion you felt for an animal, for example a pet. Remember this as a time of relative peace and happiness. Although we often direct compassion toward our loved ones during times of distress, this exercise involves using imagery to evoke a feeling that is separate from difficult emotions. As you imagine feeling kindness and compassion toward others, see whether you can imagine yourself expanding as the warmth and care of your intention grows. Imagine that you're becoming a wiser, emotionally stronger, and warmer person with each inhale and exhale. As you become more mature and resilient with every breath, recognize that this means with each breath you have more to give—that with each moment you're becoming more helpful, open, and wise. How does this feel? What physical sensations are you having?

Now, bring your attention back to the flow of your breath, and focus on these feelings and this image for a moment longer, all the while observing your desire for this person to be happy, to be filled with compassion, to be peaceful and at ease, and to be well.

What's your tone of voice like? What expression is on your face? How's your body moving and reacting to your feelings and to the feelings of the other person? Take some time to enjoy the sense of pleasure you may derive from being helpful and caring. Remember to smile gently, and as you breathe in and out, allow yourself to notice the sensation of compassion flowing out of you so that it reaches this person whom you care so deeply about. Imagine your compassion touching his heart. Imagine the burden of his suffering is lifted little by little with every breath. With your next natural exhale, sense again the compassion flowing out of you, and sense joy and peace flowing into the person you're sharing kindness with. With your next natural exhale, let go of this representation of the other person and draw your attention simply to the experience of compassion in yourself. Recognize where in the body your open and heartfelt desire to share kindness and helpfulness presents itself. Allow yourself to rest in this feeling of loving-kindness for others, feeling the presence of compassion for others as it flows through you. Stay with this sensation for a few moments more.

If your attention wanders at any point, simply pay mindful attention to where it has gone and then refocus by bringing part of your attention to your next natural inhale and to the exercise at hand.

After some time, when you've remained in the presence of this warmth and kindness for a number of minutes, you can return your awareness to your feet on the floor; then to your position in the chair; then to your back, straight and supported; and ultimately to the top of your head. When you feel you're ready, exhale and let go of this exercise, giving yourself some credit for having engaged in this practice. You may wish to jot down some of your observations in your Weekly Mindfulness Practice Record or journal. If you're working with a therapist, a meditation teacher, or other people who are practicing compassionate mind training, you may wish to share some of your observations and experiences with them.

Many people who struggle with anxiety have had troubling emotional experiences involving their caregivers; others will struggle with anxiety-related emotions that relate to their negative experience of affiliation. This in turn leads to fearful and destructive behavior and difficulty creating a compassionate self. Such a fear of self-compassion and a lack of experience of kindness can be a powerful and poignant obstacle to the activation of our capacity to regulate our emotions.

As a result, CFT practitioners understand that it's best to learn compassion in small steps, gradually building a capacity to evoke self-compassion, and to activate positive, calming emotions when faced with elevated levels of anxiety. So, in this book we began with exercises that involve relatively small steps, which can be seen as a sort of hierarchy of exposure to compassion itself; after the initial training in mindfulness, you began to explore mindfulness training by using visualization, when you imagined a safe place you could return to in your mind when you're feeling distressed or anxious. The next step involved the construction of your image of a compassionate self whose qualities include such things as empathy, tolerance to distress, wisdom, patience, and the ability to be calm and to show kindness. By focusing on your compassionate self, you're getting in touch with your affiliative soothing system and training yourself to access this system whenever and wherever you need it. Following the construction and awakening of a compassionate self, you learned how self-compassion may be evoked by using imagination and memories to experience compassion flowing in, as well as to experience compassion flowing out. In these practices, the use of imagination was directly connected to your emotional experiences and activated your emotion-regulation system.

Our final imagery exercise involves creating an image of a compassionate ideal whom you can relate to through visualization and who becomes an inner helping hand and shoulder to lean on during times of stress and anxiety.

Creating and Encountering the Compassionate Ideal

Start by practicing your soothing-rhythm breathing. Take a few minutes to bring mindful, self-compassionate awareness to the flow of your breath. In this moment, allow your awareness to follow the natural, calming rhythm of your breath as it helps you focus on the present moment.

Drop your tongue from the roof of your mouth, relax, and feel the muscles of your face form a gentle smile. As you have in your other exercises, adjust your posture to feel grounded, supported, and as though it embodies the qualities of dignity and supple stability.

You may wish to think about your compassionate, safe place where you can feel yourself surrounded by a sense of emotional warmth and where you can begin to form the image of your compassionate ideal.

The image of your compassionate ideal is built up, gradually, from elements of your imagination and experience. The image can be very personal; it's meant to have significance for you, and you alone. If your compassionate ideal changes over the course of this exercise, fine. You may even develop more than one image. For now, though, settling into the present moment, draw your attention to the qualities that you'd like to see in this particularly compassionate ideal.

Begin by asking yourself what qualities really make you feel cared for, protected, and soothed. And remember, this is an *ideal* image that you're breathing life into; you don't need to be concerned about realistic expectations. This ideal is your own personal mythical being, closest friend, superhero, or guardian angel. Sometimes people use the image of the ideal parent, but keep in mind this image will never criticize you or be angry with you. You're creating a compassionate ideal based on the qualities you wished to encounter in the Experiencing Compassion Flowing In exercise.

One quality you might wish for in your compassionate ideal is a deep reservoir of inner strength. Another is the ability to tolerate and contain anxiety and distress without being overwhelmed and with immovable compassion and calm, even in the presence of great pain and fear.

Your compassionate ideal embodies a deep commitment to alleviate your anxiety and pain; it takes pleasure and satisfaction when you experience joy and happiness. The greatest desire of your compassionate ideal is to help calm your suffering and anxiety and to bring you peace, warmth, and contentment.

Your compassionate ideal represents and personifies wisdom and understands that life is very hard and that none of us chooses to struggle with anxiety, an emotion common to everyone. Emotional pain and fear is our common bond, and you can sense that this compassionate ideal has learned through experience that suffering is not our fault. After all, we didn't choose to be here, nor did we choose to evolve with such very complicated brains, filled with strong and confusing emotions and motivations. We didn't choose our personal histories or our painful memories. Knowing all of this, your compassionate ideal truly understands the complexity of the life you face and is filled with abundant kindness and a broad, accepting perspective.

When you're in the presence of this compassionate ideal, you can sense the great warmth that this image embodies. You can feel patience, understanding, caring, and kindness emanating from the presence of this image. Your compassionate ideal is also absolutely accepting of you, exactly as you are, here and now. This compassionate presence never condemns you, never judges you, and holds you in perfect and unwavering kindness, now and forever, without condition or reservation.

As your mind encounters each of these qualities, allow them and the sense of them to wash over you as you follow your breath into and out of your body.

As you continue to form the image of your compassionate ideal, notice what form this guiding presence takes. Is it perhaps a human being, a mythical creature, or an animal? Perhaps your compassionate image represents aspects of nature, such as a pure, radiant light, or the ocean. How old or young is this image—is it youthful and innocent, is it older and wise, or is it ageless? Is it male, female, or neither? What might this image be wearing? Would it be dressed or adorned with colors or textures that feel soothing? Add to this image as much as you desire and allow yourself to connect with your compassionate ideal's ultimate and absolute intention, which is to be completely committed to the alleviation of your suffering. Your compassionate ideal wants nothing in this world so much as for you to find happiness, live in peace, and experience well-being and joyfulness, in this moment.

As you allow this image to form in your mind, rest in the soothing flow of your breath and take a moment to let your imagination simply be in the company of this compassionate ideal, which is directing all of its kindness and attentions toward you. As your breath follows its own rhythm, allow your mind to repeat the following words, which come from your compassionate ideal: *May you be filled with compassion and kindness; may you be well; may you be peaceful and at ease; may you be free from suffering; may you be happy.*

Imagine these words flowing from your compassionate ideal into you with each inhale, and then, with each exhale, release any tension or struggle within yourself. Simply let go. Stay with this image of your compassionate ideal, this recitation, and this flow of your breath, remaining in the calming presence of your compassionate ideal for as long as feels right to you.

When you're ready, with your next natural exhale, gradually allow this image to fade, and return your attention to the soothing rhythm of your breath. When the time is right, give yourself some credit for having engaged with this practice of creating a compassionate ideal, and let go of this exercise altogether with your next natural exhale.

USING COMPASSIONATE IMAGERY IN EVERYDAY LIFE

The kind of gradual practice represented by the preceding exercises can develop your ability to calmly, compassionately, and courageously face your anxiety, worry, and fear; however, you aren't limited to working with compassionate imagery purely through formal exercises. For example, once you've begun to have a clear and accessible image of your compassionate self or your compassionate ideal, you may find it helpful to pause for a few moments when you're feeling distressed or anxious, in order to bring one of these images to mind. You might then imagine yourself having a soothing and encouraging conversation with your compassionate self, feeling the emotional tone of warmth and helpfulness that this part of you brings into your mind and heart. Responding in this way will allow you to, over time, build a new range of responses to anxiety. This also lays the foundation for compassionate thinking and the range of thought-based techniques that we use in CFT.

8

Compassionate Thinking

MOVING FROM THE ANXIOUS MIND TOWARD COMPASSIONATE THINKING

As we explored together in the first part of this book, anxiety involves the activation of the threat-detection system and involves attention, physical sensations, thoughts, and emotions. Our thoughts can become extremely negative and provoke even more fear and dread when we're anxious. These thoughts can stir up a common form of anxiety-driven thinking typically referred to as worry, which involves generating representations of things that could go wrong in the future, usually in a "what if" format: *What if I lose my job? What if I get cancer? What if I can't make any friends?* As discussed, the ability to imagine a range of possible threats and prepare a number of protection responses has much to do with how we've evolved to deal with threats. When hypothetical risks and dangers show up, our threat-detection system may treat them as real; similarly, when these worries arrive they can stir up or compound distressing emotions and control our behavior. Our attention narrows to focus on these thoughts, and we may then have a narrower range of possible behaviors available to us. This kind of thinking may have had its evolutionary usefulness, but it isn't often very helpful for us now.

Compassionate thinking brings your compassionate self to the aid of your anxious self by helping you see things, or think about things, in a different way. Your anxious self might be quick to jump to conclusions, because of its orientation to being "better safe than sorry." It will also be bound to your memories; so if you've had a bad experience in the past, your anxious self will remind you about that and reactivate those feelings of fear and dread. However, when your compassionate attention alerts you to the onset of anxiety, you can choose to move toward compassionate thinking to help you face your worry, fear, and panic.

Let's take a closer look at this process to see how you can actually work with compassionate thinking to take care of yourself when you respond to anxiety.

Imagine that you're stuck in heavy traffic, which is causing you to run late for an important meeting. Suddenly you start to feel panicked; your stomach tightens and maybe you have a tingling in your fingers. At the same time, your anxiety generates the following thoughts:

- *Oh my god, I'm starting to feel bad; I might be sick.*

- *What happens if I have to throw up and I have to lean out of the car?*

- *I'm stuck in a traffic jam and I can't pull over!*

- *This is terrible—unbearable. What are they going to think of me at the meeting? I've been trying to set up this deal for weeks, and now this happens! What if it falls through?*

- *Oh no, my heart is racing. What if I'm having a heart attack and die?*

Actually, just writing this makes me feel a bit of anxiety in my chest. Sometimes it's scary to even think about a situation like this one. But what would you do, how would you react, and how would you feel if you engaged your compassionate self right now?

First, let's focus on practicing soothing-rhythm breathing, which will help your breath slow down. Just for a moment, find a place to rest in your breath. When we get anxious, we tend to speed up our breathing, and it becomes shallow because of the tension in our bodies. This can also evoke some of the other physiological symptoms of feeling anxious, such as tingling of the skin, nausea, and light-headedness. You're not using soothing-rhythm breathing in an attempt to banish your anxiety or struggle against it in an effort for control; you're simply preparing the way for your compassionate self and coming into the moment with a warm-hearted acceptance, as much as you can.

Next, take on the posture of dignity, and create a friendly facial expression, even if you don't really feel like it. Imagine being in the safe place where you've been practicing your exercises. Does that help? Imagine your compassionate self in the safe place and then moving from that safe place to where you are now, in this moment. This is the compassionate self who is going to help you as you face this situation. Now think about how you'd like best to be able to respond to this anxiety. How would you understand it, tolerate it, and get through it? You can't magically make traffic start moving—wishful thinking doesn't usually work to cope with anxiety, particularly in the long term. It's far better to learn how to tolerate anxiety, ride it like a wave, and recognize that you don't need to be scared of it even though it's frightening. For the moment, imagine yourself coping as the ideal, compassionate self. What would this compassionate and wise self be thinking? Would it be calm, and would it try to help you also be calm? Try some of these thoughts and see what you think:

- *I've felt anxiety like this before, many times, and I know that I can feel claustrophobic—I recognize these feelings as my threat-detection system doing what it has evolved to do. It's unpleasant for me, but it's a part of life.* (Always remember to validate what you feel. Recognize the suffering.)

- *These anxiety feelings are not my fault—they're partly related to the way my brain is built, and also to things that have happened to me in the past. Maybe I'm experiencing panic now because my life is very stressful at the moment and so my anxiety threshold is weakened.* (Understand the context and remind yourself of the nature of panic.)

- *Many people suffer panic attacks—not just me.* (As much as you hate panicking, remind yourself that you suffer from it along with many millions of other people. You're not alone.)

- *I've had these feelings many times before, and they do pass and subside—I can bring to mind times when I've panicked in the past and when it's then gone away. Let me just hold that memory of successfully coping in mind.* (See your panic as part of life's journey and that it comes and goes.)

- *When people are panicked, it's very common for them to believe something terrible is going to happen as a result, but, in fact, panicking doesn't kill you. Our bodies are designed to cope with feelings of panic. There's no evidence that people who've suffered from panic attacks are more at risk of dying from heart attacks than other people.* (Hold in mind the evidence about the difference between feelings of panic and having heart attacks.)

So you see, the key process here involves validating your feelings while being kind to yourself and recognizing them as unpleasant. You don't need to tell yourself that you're being silly or neurotic or pathetic or that you just have to grin and bear it, because thoughts like these are not very kind or supportive. Also, while it's understandable if you get irritated and angry with your anxiety (*Why does this have to happen now? What the hell is the matter with me? I hate feeling like this!*), your task in evoking your compassionate self is to be at your *most supportive*.

Sometimes, though, learning not to panic can be helpful, and one way to do this is to connect with your sense of wisdom, authority, and a real commitment to try to be helpful, not on trying to come up with the most accurate assessment of the situation. Imagine yourself as if you were hovering slightly above the anxiety and then expanding to capture the anxiety. Can you see how much bigger you are than the anxiety? When you do, you'll be able to watch your experience of panic unfold in safety.

Sometimes it can be useful to imagine how you'd help a friend who was in a state of panic; however, if you're unsure of how to help yourself, it can be difficult to know what to say to a friend. But if you learn how to be kind to yourself, and to support yourself with acceptance, you can become understanding, kind, and supportive to others also.

So run through these thoughts in your mind, but always keep those feelings of deep understanding, courage, kindness, and warmth, because your compassionate self knows how scary panic is. Your compassionate self won't be dismissive of how you're feeling or what you're thinking.

Here's an experiment: Read through the alternative thoughts set out above, as if you were testing out whether you believe them. Rate them from 0 to 10, with 0 being very hard to believe (not helpful at all in an anxiety situation) and 10 being very easy to believe (would relieve your anxiety).

Now, close your eyes and engage your soothing-rhythm breathing, adopt a soft facial expression, and imagine talking with a friend in a firm but kind tone of voice. Sit upright in the chair with your back straight and supported, and engage with your sense of dignity and strength. Next spend a moment or two imagining seeing your compassionate self from the outside. See how you stand, how you talk, how you look, and how people relate to you. Then bring yourself back into being this compassionate self, with as much warmth and kindness as you can. Next, refocus on those alternative thoughts very slowly indeed, and on the genuine desire to be helpful with the difficult feelings you're experiencing—don't rush it, and continue to breathe rhythmically and calmly.

What did you notice? Did you find yourself feeling more grounded and more able to tolerate anxiety when you used your compassionate self to help you? Remember, every time you make this compassionate and courageous effort to cope with frightening thoughts, you're strengthening your connection to your compassionate self.

BRINGING COMPASSIONATE THINKING CLOSER INTO CONTACT WITH WORRIES AND ANXIOUS THOUGHTS

When we use the word "worry," we're referring to the way the anxious mind will generate predictions about what might go wrong in the future. Our threat-detection system cooks up worries in the form of "what if" questions that can provoke a great deal more anxiety and fear in us. See whether any of these "what ifs" sound familiar to you from your own experience of worried thinking:

- *What if I never find a job?*

- *What if nobody wants to date me or be with me?*

- *What if I get sick?*

- *What if I lose my retirement savings?*

Of course, the anxious mind is very good at generating anxiety-provoking predictions of possible threats. All too often, our emotional brains then respond to these imaginary threats as if they were real, so our physical sensations, feelings, and behavior come to be dominated by our worries. Let's take a look at how compassionate thinking can help us address our worries and anxious thoughts in clear and useful ways.

First, it helps if we consider what our anxious mind is actually focused on and explore our thoughts from flexible perspectives. To do this, we can ask ourselves a series of questions. In traditional cognitive therapy this is sometimes called guided discovery. Here are some examples:

- *What's going through my mind when I'm anxious?*

- *How does my anxious self see the world, and what does it think about the current situation?*

- *What's my anxious self most anxious about, right now?*

As you begin to practice this kind of questioning, it's sometimes useful to write these thoughts down and then imagine your compassionate self, with its wisdom, sense of authority, calmness, and genuine desire to care. How would your compassionate self respond to these thoughts? How would the presence of self-compassion guide your discovery?

For example, imagine that you have to give a presentation to your colleagues. The prospect of this stirs up your anxiety, and your mind begins to generate worry and fantasies of the presentation going horribly wrong. You ask yourself: *What if I just freeze? What if I really screw this up and wind up getting fired?* You might hear your mind saying such things, and because you're so close to the experience, it seems as if these thoughts present real threats and may come true, instead of being *events in the mind*; however, you're learning now to give yourself a chance to step back by asking yourself, *What is my mind telling me right now?* After all, we don't need to believe everything that we think! We can, instead, bring our thoughts before the witness of our compassionate self and in this way shift our perspective.

It can be helpful to write down the distressing thoughts you have in response to stress and anxiety; in this way you can generate alternative thoughts, new ways of responding, in line with compassionate thinking. There's a worksheet later in this chapter called the Compassionate-Thought Record to help you do just that. This chapter will teach you a range of techniques to move toward compassionate thinking. It's important to remember, though, that when we aim to think differently in compassionate mind training, we aren't looking to just dispute our thoughts, test their validity, or become more rational; the aim is to develop a self-compassionate, mindful experience of warmth, self-acceptance, and kindness.

TECHNIQUES FOR ENGAGING COMPASSIONATE THINKING

As you might expect, compassionate thinking is interwoven with many other compassionate attributes and skills. It necessarily involves building on our training in compassionate attention and compassionate imagery. Let's take a look at an example of how compassionate thinking can be applied to an anxiety-provoking situation. Imagine that my client Jennifer, the preschool teacher, is going for an interview for a new position as a history teacher at a middle school. This exciting opportunity represents a big step up for her. So, despite her apprehension about interview situations, Jennifer has decided to take a chance and apply for the position. She arrives early for the interview and sits in the waiting room for a few minutes before the appointed time. She begins to notice that she's feeling apprehensive, nervous, and fidgety. Her mind is beginning to race with worries and predictions of failure; however, Jennifer has been practicing her compassionate-thinking exercises and begins to respond to these feelings by taking a few mindful, soothing-rhythm breaths. She allows herself to rest in her breath and asks herself, *What is my anxious self/mind telling me right now?* Stepping back from the flow of her anxious thoughts, Jennifer is able to notice that she's having the fearful thought *I'm going to mess up this interview and it's going to be a total disaster!* But because she has gathered herself into the calm flow of soothing-rhythm breathing, she's better able to recognize this thought as one associated with her feelings of anxiety and her threat-detection system, rather than as a fact. After all, she's prepared for the interview, and she has the experience and credentials that would make her suitable for the position.

With part of her attention still focused on the gentle rhythm of her breath, she next imagines herself *as* her compassionate self and asks herself what this wise, kind, and helpful aspect of herself might say in this situation. Beyond this, she might also have a sense of what it would feel like, emotionally, to be in the presence of this compassionate friend. Sitting in the waiting area, Jennifer imagines that her compassionate self tells her: *Jennifer, it's completely natural that you'd have some feelings of anxiety or fear in this situation. Job interviews can be anxiety provoking for all of us. We've evolved with such complex minds, and our anxiety can be activated so quickly, so this is not your fault, and you're okay just the way you are. Remember that you've prepared for a long time and that you're competent, caring, and knowledgeable. When you think about it, you actually do have a job already, and you're doing very well there. As much as you can, just make space for the ups and downs of what you feel, and hold yourself in kindness and care, just as I do.* After imagining these words, Jennifer recalls the sensations she has experienced during the Experience Compassion Flowing In exercise and connects with a sense of mindful self-compassion. She recognizes that by stepping out of her comfort zone to come to this job interview, she has begun to engage in compassionate behavior. She's being kind to herself, being courageous, and putting up with feeling anxious in order to move in a new and meaningful direction.

Developing the skill of compassionate thinking takes some practice, and that practice can take place throughout the day, as a natural part of your daily life. Sometimes this practice can take place in a structured way, through the use of the Compassionate-Thought Record. At other times, you might simply use your creativity and wisdom, without the use of the Compassionate-Thought Record and without writing anything down. Part of the aim in compassionate mind training is for you to learn and internalize these compassionate-thinking skills and build your compassionate attributes, so that your new, more helpful response to anxiety becomes automatically and inherently more mindful and self-compassionate.

Let's take a look at three approaches to developing compassionate thinking. These eventually will become a part of your broader range of responses to anxiety. They share some common ideas, and they all share the common aim of helping you activate and embody your capacity for self-acceptance, kindness, warmth, and a deep sense of safety and contentment in the present moment. These three approaches are (a) compassionate responding, (b) distinguishing self-criticism from compassionate self-correction, and (c) compassionate defusion.

COMPASSIONATE RESPONDING

In CFT the way to change your response to anxiety is to first notice the flow of anxious and negative thoughts as they move through your consciousness and then come up with alternative, more positive thoughts that adopt a more compassionate perspective, allowing balance, self-care, and movement toward compassionate behavior. You ask yourself questions, and shift your perspective in ways that evoke the emotional tone of your compassionate self and connect you with a sense of warmth, wisdom, and inner resilience.

You may find it helpful to write down some of your observations as you practice these exercises, and notice how the alternative responses affect your feelings.

The Compassionate Double Standard

You can do this exercise anywhere, whenever you notice that you've become anxious or are feeling distressed.

First ask yourself, *What's going through my mind right now?* See whether you can stand back from the flow of your thinking and, in a sentence or two, capture the thoughts going through your mind. For example, if you were stuck in traffic and as a result were running late for work, you might feel stress and pressure building up. That would be a good time to take a moment to stand back and ask yourself compassionately what you're thinking in that moment. You might notice that you had been worrying and that the "what ifs" had begun to pop up: *What if I'm late? If I'm going to be late, then this is going to be a total disaster. I'm going to be in huge trouble. I've screwed everything up!*

The next step is to ask yourself an important question: *What would I say to a good friend who was faced with this same situation?* If your best friend called you while she was stuck in traffic and panicked about running late, you might respond by saying "That kind of situation can be so frustrating. As much as you can, remember that the traffic is not your fault and is out of your control. You're probably one of hundreds of people stuck on the same route. If you can, let yourself off the hook on this, and just call your office to let them know you're stuck." In speaking kindly and supportively to your friend in this situation, you'd be helping your friend both validate her distress and move beyond her anxiety and find the best solution to the problem. Further, you'd be providing the support and calming influence that arrives with the activation of our experience of compassion from others, through our contentment and soothing emotion-regulation system.

As the name of that exercise implies, we often apply harsher rules and standards to ourselves than we would to others. Our inner critic and threat-detection system can be activated by stress, and that can result in reacting to our threatening, worrisome thoughts in less helpful ways than if we were engaging with our compassionate selves. This additional pressure can ramp up our experience of shame and anxiety. Looking at your situation and your automatic thinking as if it were happening to a friend, and then responding to the anxious thoughts and worries with compassion, support, and care, can help you be just that kind of supportive friend to yourself. You can adopt a more helpful, compassionate, and kind attitude toward yourself. You can view the situation through the lens of your compassionate mind and respond with balance, patience, and support.

The next exercise also begins with the simple act of noticing where your mind is, and what it's doing, in a particular moment of anxiety.

Examining, from a Place of Compassion, the Costs and Benefits of Buying into a Thought

You can do this exercise anywhere, whenever you're in distress or you notice you're experiencing the physical sensations or emotions involved in anxiety. Initially, do this exercise on paper. Then, once you've become experienced at doing this exercise, you might want to do it just in your imagination.

Ask yourself, *What's going through my mind right now?* After noticing the thought, write it down at the top of a sheet of paper. Begin to ask yourself, *What are the advantages and disadvantages of buying into this thought?* Draw a vertical line down the center of the paper, and write "Costs" at the top of one half, and "Benefits" at the top of the other. List the costs and benefits of believing this thought, and then review what you've written. Ask yourself: *Do the costs of buying into this thought outweigh the benefits? Does it help me to buy into this thought? If I did believe this, how would I behave? Do I want to hand my behavior, and my life, over to this kind of thinking?* You might consider how your compassionate self would advise you in this.

Taking a few soothing-rhythm breaths, activating compassionate attention, and bringing your compassionate self to mind, you might ask that kind and helpful part of you whether believing this thought will serve your valued aims and will lead you to self-compassionate behavior. If you decide that it's more costly than beneficial to believe in or act on this thought, you can bring acceptance and compassion to your experience of the present moment, see the thought for what it truly is—an event in the mind—and refocus your mindful attention on a compassionate alternative thought that will help you behave in a compassionate, effective, and kind way.

The next exercise is adapted from a cognitive therapy exercise that encourages you to adopt a new perspective on your thoughts and feelings by reimagining the situation you're in. Again, it begins with a central question that helps you engage with and acknowledge your thoughts.

The Compassionate View from the Balcony

You can use this exercise any time you notice anxiety or distress building, whether it be in a particular place or situation or completely out of the blue. It may be that you notice your unpleasant emotions because of physical sensations, such as tension or nausea; at other times you may notice negative thoughts begin to swirl around. Whatever the case, allow yourself this moment of observation, and ask yourself: *What's going through my mind right now? What's my mind telling me?* or *What am I thinking in this moment?* As much as you can, see whether you can catch the thoughts as they unfold in your inner monologue, and observe them as sentences that you can jot down or repeat. For example, after an argument with a friend, you might nervously wait for your friend to call and either apologize or talk things through. Or you might be trying to build up the courage to make the call yourself. Feeling the tension in your chest and pressure in your temples, you might notice that you're feeling anxious and angry. Making space for these emotions, you could choose to ask yourself *What's my mind telling me right now?* Casting a lens on your thoughts, you might notice such statements as *She's driving me crazy!* or *I've ruined everything!*

Once you've noticed the things that your anxious mind is saying, you can begin to use your imagination and perspective to work with your distressing thoughts. Imagine that you're at a beautiful theater, and you're watching a play from one of the balconies. At one point during the play, the protagonist is acting out a moment of distress. You've been watching the play for some time now, and you've developed empathy, compassion, and warm feelings for this character. Imagine now, though, that the character you're watching is actually you. The play you're seeing is a play about exactly the same situation you find yourself in right now. Rather than watching the events and thinking the thoughts from the inside, though, you're now able to have some distance and observe how the protagonist has struggled, as all humans do, and has felt some serious anxiety.

You recognize that this is not the protagonist's fault: she didn't choose to be in this situation or ask for her anxious suffering, and she never asked to face the difficulties and challenges she's being presented with. This character has struggled and suffered, and you feel great empathy for her. You understand her pain and are moved to help her alleviate her suffering. How might you respond to the negative, anxiety-based thinking that you sometimes notice within you, in this compassionate view from the balcony?

The following worksheet is structured to help you practice compassionate thinking every day with questions that can guide you through the steps of compassionate thinking.

The Compassionate-Thought Record

Ask yourself the following questions, using the guidelines set out for thinking about and responding to them.

1. *What is the situation I find myself in?* Think about what you're doing in this moment, here and now. Where are you? Are you interacting with anyone? What do you see, hear, feel and notice around you? What are you reacting to right now? Write your response in the space below.

_____

_____

_____

_____

2. *What physical sensation(s) am I experiencing?* Turn your attention inward and notice what physical sensations you're experiencing right now. Write them in the space below. Allow yourself to make space for these experiences, mindfully engaging in the soothing-rhythm breathing practice. Allow yourself to experience this sensation or these sensations with kindness.

_____

_____

_____

_____

3. *What emotion(s) am I feeling?* Think about how, based on your sensations, you'd label the emotion(s) you're feeling now. What words would you use for your current emotion(s)? How intensely are you feeling this emotion or these emotions, on a scale from 0 to 100? Write your response in the space below.

_____

_____

_____

_____

4. *What is my mind telling me?* Think about what's going through your mind right now. What thoughts are popping into your head? Write them in the space below.

_____

_____

_____

_____

5. *Can I mindfully and compassionately make space for this experience, here and now?* This one's a rhetorical question: Continue to engage in soothing-rhythm breathing, and bring to mind an attitude of warmth and self-acceptance. Take this opportunity to learn to stay with your experience, just as it is. Follow the flow of your breath in this moment, as much as you can, making space for whatever unfolds before your mind. Know that you are more than your thoughts, emotions, and bodily sensations, and that you can let yourself recognize that you are a part of the flow of life and that this is not your fault. Recall how your compassionate self feels, and hold yourself in acceptance and kindness, right here and right now. Use the space below to write any observations you make as you do this.

_____

_____

_____

_____

6. *How might I respond through compassionate thinking?* Think about how you might best respond to your thoughts and emotions in this moment, with compassion, wisdom, and acceptance. Are you being nonjudgmental? What might help you come closer to compassionate thinking? What reactions and observations have you noticed from the perspective of compassionate thinking? Record your thoughts on this theme in the space below.

_____

_____

_____

_____

7. *After engaging in compassionate thinking while feeling anxious and distressed, what do I notice about my current emotions, thoughts, body sensations, and behavioral urges?* Think about what's happening for you right now in this regard and write it down.

_____

_____

_____

_____

There will be some times when you can use this worksheet "in real time," writing down your responses to anxiety and other emotions as they happen. At other times, you won't have that opportunity, but can complete the worksheet later in the day, looking back on an event and then rehearsing how you might respond when a similar event happens, or reflecting on how you were able to use compassionate thinking to help you cope with your anxiety during the situation. With practice, this written format will help you shift from an anxious perspective to a compassionate one automatically. Feel free to experiment with this worksheet and to share your observations with your therapist or with people you trust who are helping you on your journey. Alternatively, you may wish to keep some of these observations private.

It's important to remember that all the skills and attributes of the compassionate mind are connected and that your work with mindful attention and compassionate imagery has established a foundation for your work with compassionate thinking.

DISTINGUISHING SELF-CRITICISM FROM COMPASSIONATE SELF-CORRECTION

For many of us, self-criticism is a large part of our inner life. Our learning histories may have involved experiences that taught us to believe negative messages about ourselves and cause us to feel shameful or not worthy. Such experiences might include being a child of abusive parents, being bullied, or other forms of physical or sexual abuse. Perhaps we've experienced neglect or abandonment. When our caregivers treat us with contempt, cruelty, or violence, we might then react to the experience of a relationship with an activation of our threat-detection system. If we look for compassion and safety from others but are instead punished or mistreated, this can lead to our learning to block or fear the experience of compassion and affiliation. This can also lead to an overactivation of our threat-detection system, a pervasive experience of shame and self-loathing, and an active inner critic.

It seems that we're designed to blame ourselves when we have difficulty dealing with our fears and with our perception of threats, which can feel overwhelming. Our problem-solving minds try to find some source of control, some method of finding certainty in the midst of anxiety and danger, and we often blame ourselves if we're not able to find that source or not able to take control. We've evolved to draw on whatever resources are at hand to make ourselves safer.

Remember that through compassionate mind training you're aiming to shift the center of gravity of your experience from threat-detection emotion regulation toward the activation of your compassion-based system. Because emotions, thoughts, and behaviors are interwoven, when you operate from a place of compassion, your thinking takes on a different character and emotional tone, as does your behavior.

You didn't choose your evolutionary history, nor did you choose the learning history that has led you to struggle with anxiety and shame. Developing the compassionate mind begins in the present moment, with the recognition that the situation you find yourself in is simply not your fault, and with a choice to accept yourself fully, just as you are, without any condemnation or judgment and with compassion for your struggles. When I introduce this idea to my clients, many resist it strongly. They believe that if they accept themselves fully and see their anxiety and suffering as not their fault, they'll no longer care about how they treat themselves or others. For some, it seems, the idea of compassionate self-acceptance involves self-indulgence, selfishness, or a lack of responsibility. In fact, these qualities are not at all part of how the compassionate mind functions. Research has demonstrated that people who have a high degree of self-compassion are actually less self-indulgent than others.[1] To operate from the compassionate mind is to have a deep appreciation of the suffering of both others and ourselves. We recognize our common humanity and are moved to do something to alleviate this suffering. This involves consciously taking responsibility for our actions and plotting a course of compassionate behavior for ourselves that can live up to the heartfelt aspirations that emerge from our compassionate selves.

Many of my clients also believe that they need to be harshly self-critical if they're going to better themselves: that if they bully or beat themselves up, they might whip themselves into shape and become more motivated to take charge of their lives. This is a common belief. Perhaps you have memories of teachers or coaches who tried to motivate you through derision or harsh criticism. It may have seemed to work, but in fact this kind of verbal punishment rarely produces a positive behavior change. Such punishment often results in a decreased frequency of positive behavior, not an increase of it. More often than not, our attacks on ourselves, in the guise of "whipping ourselves into shape," actually have the effect of narrowing our range of behaviors and increasing our anxiety, rather than helping us live our lives more calmly, evenly, and effectively. If you allow yourself to be engulfed by your anxious thoughts and feelings, and if you surrender your behavior to your fear or to avoidance, you're not actually living from a compassionate intention; however, if on the contrary you train your mind to respond with compassionate thinking, adopting compassionate self-correction rather than verbally attacking or criticizing yourself, you'll be better able to respond to your experience of anxiety and shame. Training your compassionate mind can help you experience positive emotions more readily, overcome anxiety, and more effectively pursue your goals.

The table below outlines some of the differences between self-criticism and compassionate self-correction.

Compassionate self-correction is focused on:	Judgmental self-criticism is focused on:
• The desire to improve • Growth and enhancement • Looking forward • Generosity, encouragement, support and kindness • Building on positives (e.g., seeing what you've done well and considering what you've learned from other things that would benefit from improvement) • Positive attributes and specific qualities of the self • Hope for success • Possibilities for increasing the chances of engaging with the compassionate mind	• The desire to condemn and punish • Punishing past errors and often looking backward • Meanness, anger, frustration, contempt, and disappointment • Deficits and fear of exposure • Fear of failure • Possibilities of avoidance and withdrawal
Note the example of an encouraging, supportive teacher (below).	Note the example of a critical teacher (below).

From *The Compassionate Mind*, Gilbert, 2009; reprinted with permission.

Compassionate self-correction is grounded in the desire to alleviate suffering and to help us realize our hearts' deepest desire to be able to behave as we'd wish to. Paul Gilbert has illustrated this difference by contrasting the styles of two imaginary teachers—one critical, the other encouraging and supportive—each working with young children who are struggling to perform at grade level.

The critical teacher believes that it's beneficial to focus on the deficits and faults that a child might have and that teasing and chiding her pupils for their mistakes will help them learn. Her students come to fear and resent her when she looks over their shoulders at their work, and she herself spends a lot of time feeling angry and anxious about how her students are performing.

The encouraging, supportive teacher pays a lot of attention to the strengths and talents that her students demonstrate. Her expectations are clear, and she gives specific behavioral feedback to the children about how they could improve their performance. She does not chide them or tease them. She's encouraging, warm, strong, and wise.

Did you have teachers like this when you were at school? Which one did you study harder for? Which one did you prefer? Which teacher might have shaped your sense of self-confidence and, as a result, helped build your capacity to respond to frustration and anxiety with warmth and ability to tolerate distress?

Compassionate self-correction is not about denying your mistakes or weaknesses; instead, it focuses on radical self-acceptance: accepting your fallibility, your frailty, and your suffering, all of which are essential aspects of your common humanity. Such acceptance also involves a deep kindness and appreciation of your desire to alleviate your suffering, to grow, to develop, and to realize your valued aims. As Gilbert wrote:

> Compassionate self-correction is based on being open-hearted and honest about our mistakes with a genuine wish to improve and learn from them. No one wakes up in the morning and thinks to themselves, "Oh, I think I will make a real cock-up of things today, just for the hell of it." Most of us would like to do well, most of us would like to avoid mistakes, most of us would like to avoid being out of control with our temper. We need to recognize that our genuine wish is to improve.[2]

The following exercises represent a few methods for overcoming self-criticism through developing your capacity for compassionate self-correction. You can experiment with them as part of your compassionate mind training practice and record them in your Weekly Mindfulness Practice Record or journal. As with all of the techniques here, feel free to approach them gently and with a spirit of curiosity. Part of the way in which we cultivate our capacity for compassion is to gradually build new ways of responding to anxiety, at a pace that works for us. Along this path, we discover which techniques speak to us and help us move toward greater acceptance, mindfulness, and flexibility. It's a good idea for you to record some observations in your Weekly Mindfulness Practice Record or journal about your responses to the different exercises, so that you might be able to follow a course of personal growth and healing that feels right for you.

The first exercise involves noticing the different parts of yourself, particularly your anxious mind and your compassionate mind, and then drawing a contrast between the two. You'll use a form of role-playing to create a dialogue between these aspects of your self. By doing this, you can feel what it's like when your anxious self speaks to you, and then experience how dramatically different this is from when your compassionate self speaks. In addition, this will help you practice activating your compassion system, which can help you cope with your fear and anxiety.

Two Chairs

For this exercise you'll need two chairs, which should be placed facing one another. As you begin, sit in one chair, and imagine that you're looking at a mirror image of yourself in the other chair. Take a moment and connect with your feelings of anxiety and self-critical thoughts and then speak directly to this other image, as if you were the personification of the anxious and self-critical part of yourself. Your words will involve shamefulness, worry, and bullying. You might be familiar with this kind of dialogue already, with prior experiences of similar thoughts. When you're ready, speak to the empty chair, all the while continuing to imagine that you're facing yourself and remembering that you're speaking purely from your anxious, self-critical mind and are giving a voice to your threat-detection system. Speak your fears, your self-criticism, and your worries out loud. Let yourself say things that you might not be comfortable saying typically. Feel free to verbalize your anxiety, your shame, and your self-criticism as openly as you can. Continue doing this for a few minutes and then, when you're ready, allow yourself to stop speaking. Take a moment and settle into your chair, letting some silence pass after you've spoken.

Next—and again, when you're ready—rise up and take a seat in the opposite chair. Close your eyes and allow yourself to settle into a few mindful breaths, resting in your soothing-rhythm breathing. Bring to mind the image of your compassionate self and allow a gentle smile to form on your face. Make sure you're sitting in a grounded and dignified posture and then call to mind thoughts of acceptance, forgiveness, openness, warmth, and kindness. Allow these thoughts to become physical sensations, perhaps with a feeling of warmth around your heart, or with a broadening of your smile. If it's helpful, you can even place your hands over your heart for a few moments as you follow your breath and hold the image of your compassionate self in your mind. Now, open your eyes and look at the chair before you and begin to speak completely from your mindfulness and compassion, and acknowledge that you're speaking with your anxious self. You are not chiding or bullying or criticizing; instead, you acknowledge and accept the fear of your imaginary self sitting opposite you, and you speak with wisdom, emotional strength, kindness, and the ability to tolerate the distress of this anxious self. For example, you might say "I understand how difficult this experience is for you. You are very frightened; you aren't sure whether this experience will be worthwhile. It is hard, and you are anxious, and I get that. But please remember that it is not your fault. I hold you in kindness, and have a real wish for your happiness and well-being. It is okay for you to feel this way." Stay with this compassionate voice for a few minutes more and then, when it feels right, close your eyes, and with your next natural exhale let go of the exercise altogether. When you open your eyes, bring your attention back into the room and allow yourself some credit for courageously engaging with this practice.

The Two Chairs exercise can seem a bit strange or tricky at first, but with a little practice you can begin to learn what it's like to deliberately activate your compassionate mind and to respond with compassion and self-correction when you experience fear, anxiety, and self-criticism arising within you. With regular practice, compassionate self-correction becomes something automatic in you. Your range of possible responses to self-criticism can broaden, and you can find a new freedom to bring self-compassion into the present moment as you face your anxiety and self-criticism from a place of safety, strength, and wisdom.

The next exercise will involve writing a letter to yourself from the perspective of a deeply compassionate, wise, and unconditionally accepting person. If you feel comfortable doing so, you can imagine yourself as this loving, kind presence. This voice within you is an expression of your innate loving-kindness and intuitive wisdom.

Writing a Compassionate Letter to Yourself

To prepare, set aside some time when you can engage in this exercise without interruption and without hurry. Find a space that feels private and safe and where you have a surface to write on. You could use some of your good stationery and one of your good pens, or simply use a pencil and a clean 8½ by 11 sheet of paper.

Be seated and take a minute or two to engage in mindful awareness of the flow of your breath. Feel the soles of your feet touching the ground; make sure your back is straight and supported; overall, you should be comfortable. Focus on your soothing-rhythm breathing, paying attention to the movement of your breath into and out of your body.

After a few minutes of mindful breathing, shift your attention to the flow of your thoughts; as you breathe, reflect on your current life situation. What conflicts, problems, or self-criticisms come to mind? What's your mind beginning to tell you? What emotions arise within you?

With your next natural exhale, let go of these thoughts, and on your next natural inhale shift your attention again to an image of yourself as a compassionate and wise person who possesses wisdom and emotional strength. You're unconditionally accepting of all that you are, in this moment, and you're completely nonjudgmental. Your compassionate self radiates emotional warmth. For a moment, recognize the calmness and wisdom that you possess and the physical sensations that accompany this. Recognize the strength and healing quality of a vast and deep kindness. Recognize that this loving-kindness, this powerful compassion, exists within you as an abundant reservoir of strength.

Remember to acknowledge and validate your feelings and remind yourself that there are many good reasons for the distress you're currently experiencing. Your automatic pilot has evolved to make you feel and react as you do. You were not designed to deal with the particular pressures and complexities of your current social environment. Your learning history has presented you with strong challenges and with situations that have caused you pain. Can you open yourself to a compassionate understanding that your struggle is a natural part of life and that it's not your fault?

Reflect on this, and then, when you're ready, begin to compose a letter that gives a voice to your compassionate self. Write enough to fill at least one side of your 8½ by 11 sheet of paper or both sides of your special stationery.

If you're working with a therapist, you may choose to take this letter with you to your next session, when you can read it together and reflect on the words and feelings that you've allowed yourself to express. If you're working independently, set aside some time to mindfully read this letter back to yourself with great care. Let yourself hear the words and feel the compassionate tone. If you feel the need to revise the letter, make as many subsequent drafts as you like. And please remember that each time you practice one of these CFT exercises, you're learning to come into closer contact with your compassionate emotion-regulation system, and you're developing your compassionate mind. So, feel free to practice as often as you wish, and as often as you can.

COMPASSIONATE DEFUSION

Sometimes, in order to begin a life of following valued aims and engaging in mindful and compassionate attention, thinking, and behavior, we need to break away from the mental content that represents our past learning. Your attention, thinking, and behavior may currently be directly connected, or *fused*, with certain thought processes, and you may need to gain distance, or *defuse*, from these thoughts. With self-kindness, recognition of your common humanity, and a willingness and capacity to bear distress, you can experience your thoughts as events unfolding in your mind, rather than something your anxious self must hand your life over to.

As discussed earlier in this book, when we think about or imagine something, our bodies and minds can respond as though the mental image were a real thing in the outside world. For example, if you imagine that your favorite food has been set down on the table before you, with its wonderful aroma, you might salivate or notice that you're getting hungry. Similarly, if you tell yourself *I'm going to embarrass myself at this party* or *I can't get on that airplane*, you might feel anxious or afraid. And as you begin to feel the physical effects of your anxious thoughts, you then begin to feel even more distressed. Your threat-detection emotion-regulation system becomes the captain of your soul, and you become immersed with the experience as if it were a literal event. However, because of the various mindfulness training exercises you've been practicing, you've begun to be aware of how helpful it can be to simply not take thoughts at face value; to stand back and imagine yourself as compassionate and wise; and to bring in kindness to balance your thoughts. Now you'll begin also to defuse from the way your thoughts present themselves, and to reclaim control of your behavior from your threatened-mind processes.

Practicing compassionate defusion allows you to use mindful, compassionate attention to gain perspective on the thoughts and emotions that flow through you, to separate yourself from these thoughts and consider how they're affecting you. You may benefit from becoming ever more observant of your inner experiences for what they are and not for what they try to convince you they are.

Below are a number of defusion techniques that can help you broaden your range of responses to anxious thinking. You can practice them just about anywhere, at any time.

Breaking from Identification with Thinking

Consider this: Your foot is a part of you, but it isn't all of you. When you have a dream, that dream unfolds in your mind, but it isn't "you." Similarly, the verbal thinking you do is a part of who you are, but it isn't all of who you are.

For this exercise, imagine that your mind is something outside of yourself, almost separate from you; for example, you might think *My mind is telling me that I need to stay inside today* or *Oh, my mind is doing its old, familiar pattern of worrying about my retirement.* It can also be helpful to talk through your emotional responses by saying out loud or to yourself: *My mind is telling me that I'm going to fail this test, and that's generating a flash of anxiety. This means that my body has picked up a perceived threat. I can see how this is working to make me feel butterflies in the stomach. Let's see whether I can just make space for this experience for a moment. I can notice how these thoughts are pulling my feelings around, but I'm going to return my focus to studying, as much as I can, and as often as I need to. I can contain all of this right here and now.*

By learning to stand back from your experiences, with nonjudgmental observation, you're gradually learning to defuse from the flow of mental events, rather than overidentify with them and hand your life over to anxiety. Call to mind a physical sense of warmth and the strength and wisdom that emerge from self-kindness. Understand that you're not merely the thoughts that float across your mind. You're something much bigger, much more important, and something that can contain this experience. Holding yourself in kindness, practice this defusion with the flow of your thoughts, and explore what happens.

The next technique involves linking your mental events to an object in the outside world.

Taking Your Keys with You

Grab your key ring and match each anxiety-provoking thought and feeling to one of the keys: your house key might represent worries about your romantic relationship; your car key might represent worries about your finances; your office key might represent worries about your health. It really doesn't matter which key goes with what; what matters is that you link each thought with one of the keys and experience the thought in a new context.

As you go about your day, recognize that you're carrying these sometimes troubling mental events with you, just as you're carrying your keys. You need to carry your keys in order to function in your day, just like you need to carry these thoughts. Notice the thoughts, and your ability to carry them, whenever you notice the keys. When you notice your mind returning to these familiar worries, bring part of your attention to the keys and feel them. Remember that with mindfulness, compassion, and acceptance, you can carry these thoughts just as you carry the keys, using them when you need to—in order to open and close doors that lead you in different directions throughout your life—and putting them away when you don't. Connect with your sense of compassionate tolerance of distress as you do this, recognizing that your compassionate self has sufficient warmth, wisdom, and strength to hold your anxious experience, to help you move toward what matters most to you, and to help you move away from what matters less.

The Children on the Bus[3]

Imagine that you're a bus driver. You have your uniform, your shiny dashboard, your comfortable seat, and a powerful bus at your command. This bus represents your life: all of your experiences, your challenges, and strengths have brought you to this role. You'll be driving this bus to a destination of your own choosing—a destination that represents the valued aims that you're willing to pursue. Arriving at your destination is deeply significant to you, and every inch that you travel toward this valued aim means that you've been taking your life in the right direction. It's necessary, obviously, that you keep to your route.

Like any bus driver, you're obliged to stop along the way to pick up passengers; however, the trouble with this particular journey is that some of these passengers are difficult to deal with—they're the most unruly and aggressive children you've ever encountered. Each one represents a difficult, anxiety-provoking thought or feeling that you've had to contend with over the course of your life. Some of the children might be self-criticism; others are panic and dread; still others represent worry and fear. Whatever has troubled you and distracted you from the rich possibilities of life is now hopping on your bus in the form of these unruly children, who because of their behavior seem cruel and rude: they shout insults at you and throw trash all over the place. You can hear them calling: "You're a loser!"; "Why don't you just give up? It's hopeless; we'll never get there!" One even shouts, "Stop the bus—this will never work!"

You think about stopping the bus to scold and discipline these children or throw them out, but if you did that you'd no longer be moving in the direction that matters to you. Maybe if you made a left turn and tried a different route, the children would become quiet. But this, too, would be a detour from living your life in a way that takes you toward realizing your freely chosen, valued aims. All of a sudden you realize that while you were preoccupied with devising strategies and arguments for dealing with the nagging children on the bus, you already missed a couple of turns and have lost some time. You now understand that in order to get to where you want to go, and in order to continue moving in the direction that you have chosen in life, you need to continue driving and allow these children to continue their catcalls, teasing, and nagging all the while. You can make the choice to take your life in the right direction, while just making space for all of the noise that the children generate, because you can't kick them off and you can't make them stop.

You recognize that each child represents a part of your very tricky brain that has evolved over millions of years to respond in all sorts of anxious, angry, and confusing ways to a complicated environment, and you decide to take a moment to pay attention to the road and rest in the rhythm of your breathing. When you do this, you can recognize that it's not your fault that these painful thoughts, emotions, and experiences show up. Your compassionate self, driving the bus, can make room for them all: the anxious self, the angry self, the cruel self, the jealous self, and the entire range of different aspects of your experience, all of them carrying on and vying for your attention like so many restless and mischievous children. All of this can take place as you move toward your valued aims. Importantly, you're being kind to yourself and nonjudgmental as you keep your eyes on the road.

9

Compassionate Behavior

By now you've learned that compassionate behavior involves a deep awareness of the presence of suffering in ourselves and in others, coupled with an ever-emerging aspiration to alleviate that suffering. You've looked at compassion as an aspect of our minds that has evolved to provide us with a secure base to face the challenges in life and to move toward what's truly important for us and for our loved ones. You've also learned that our compassionate minds can help us regulate our emotions and cope with anxiety. You've seen that compassionate mind training involves working with attention, imagery, thinking, and behavior as well as with emotions and motivation.

What will really move you along in overcoming anxiety is to learn to behave in new ways in relation to it. We used the example previously of learning how to drive a car, when you knew that the only way you'd improve and overcome your anxiety would be to get in the car and practice how to drive. Remember also the other things in your life that have happened as a result of your ability to face up to your anxiety (such as taking exams, going for your first job interview, or going on a first date). You got through them all and achieved things you wanted, or at least made an effort to; however, compassionate behavior isn't just what you do but how you do it.

So, for example, if you suffer from agoraphobia, part of you will want to go out into the world and overcome your fear, but another part of you will want to avoid those situations in which you might feel anxiety and panic. Compassionate behavior is about choosing to go out, even if it's difficult. Why? Because it helps you stop the suffering you cause yourself by remaining at home. You might develop a program in which you gradually try to get out, perhaps the first day going to the door to look down the road, the next day taking a few steps to the pavement or to the mailbox, and so on. The more you create an understanding voice in your mind that validates and recognizes how unpleasant anxiety is and helps you keep in mind all those things you learned about anxiety in the preceding chapters, the more you'll be able to stay with the anxiety rather than have the anxiety push you back into the house. You'll be better able to remember new responses, such as staying in contact with the present moment, paying gentle attention to your body and your breathing, and noticing when you jump to frightening conclusions or become self-critical and then acknowledging what you've noticed and refocusing on your compassionate, mindful self.

All of the behavioral changes you make using CFT are important because they build self-confidence. The key, however, is to be able to develop a behavioral program for yourself that's challenging but not overwhelming and that allows you to see that it's okay to take two steps forward and one step back as you learn to cope with your anxiety.

WHY BOTHER? CLARIFYING YOUR GOALS AND VALUED AIMS

It's clear that when we begin to engage with our anxiety, it's going to be uncomfortable for us. So the issue is: why bother? Well, bear in mind that there's no absolute rule that says you *have* to address all your anxieties. Suppose you have a fear of flying but it doesn't matter so much because you prefer to travel by car or train to better enjoy the journey, or because you prefer not to travel far and have no need to fly, or because plane travel is not something you need to do for work. In this case, you might not see any reason to overcome your fear. Many people carry with them all kinds of fears that they don't particularly want to engage with, because these fears don't really interfere with their lives. So, the first thing for you to do is clarify your valued aims and goals for working with anxiety and which parts of your anxiety and fears you need to focus on; for example, you might want to reduce your social anxiety because you want to go to college and become involved in campus life. You might want to overcome panic attacks simply because they're so unpleasant. It can be helpful to clarify what you want to achieve, especially when the going gets tough. When things seem difficult on the road to your valued aims, keep in mind what you're trying to achieve, and why. Otherwise, it can be easy to lose motivation and a sense of perspective when you become anxious.

As you look closely at ways to cultivate compassionate behavior in your life, you'll discover that identifying your heart's desire—how you truly wish to behave in the world—is a big part of activating the compassionate mind. You'll also learn how compassion can involve courage, discipline, and sacrifice as well as joy and warmth to help you experience whatever shows up for you in the present moment, be it anxiety, uncertainty, or fear of the unknown. Even in the presence of distress, engaging compassionate behavior involves perseverance and moving toward what matters most, with an expanding range of behavioral options. Compassionate behavior toward yourself may take obvious forms, such as:

- Taking care of yourself, whether by having a relaxing massage or by taking time out to spend time with people you love

- Taking care of your health, by visiting the doctor or by exercising regularly

- Taking a break from a stressful situation to relax and enjoy other activities that bring you pleasure

These are the kinds of sensible behaviors that don't really put any pressure on you and are often quite easy to do; however, facing your anxiety though self-compassionate behavior can also take less obvious yet very important forms:

- Working hard to move in directions that you value in life, like studying for exams or pursuing a career, even when this is uncomfortable and involves a sacrifice of time or energy

- Facing up to things that scare you so that you might overcome your anxiety, even though this involves distress

- Refraining from taking part in "pleasurable" activities that might harm you, such as drinking a lot of wine at a party to "take the edge off" or "calm your nerves" when you know this activity will have negative results in the long run

Let's take a closer look at some specific examples of compassionate behavior and take part in some exercises designed to help you activate your compassionate mind and motivation.

GRADUALLY DEVELOPING COMPASSIONATE BEHAVIOR

Compassionate behavior involves taking action; specifically, it involves doing things that will be helpful and supportive to those dealing with anxiety. This kind of behavior emerges from a compassionate motivation, a genuine desire to alleviate others' and our own anxious suffering. Compassionate behavior may involve soothing ourselves and others, but it also may involve moving in the direction of our valued aims, even when this means we'll confront our anxiety head-on.

Just like the development of the compassionate mind in general, the development of compassionate behavior often proceeds in a gradual, step-by-step, course. For instance, I remember a time when I decided to practice yoga regularly again after many years of only sporadic involvement. One of the things that became most clear to me once I began was that I couldn't push myself to achieve what I'd been able to when I'd practiced regularly in the past. I could stretch and breathe into a position only as deeply and as fully as was possible in that moment. It made no sense for me to try to push myself farther than I was capable of and to damage my body. In time, though, I became much better able to move through the postures and connect with my breath. This led to better energy levels and improvement in my physical health; however, I had to allow the process to happen gradually, gently, and with a blend of self-kindness, nonjudgment, and perseverance that involved the development of a form of compassionate behavior.

It takes time for us to identify and understand what matters most to us and to develop the practice of mindfulness and compassionate behavior that will help us reach our valued aims and goals.

SELF-COMPASSION IN ACTION

By now, you know that you can develop your compassionate mind to help you feel soothed, content, and calm. You also know that this involves courage, strength, and authority, which in turn provide a secure base from which you can face challenges. It's important to remember that you are not developing your mindful, compassionate self in order to allow you to curl up into a ball and hide away. Instead, you're developing a secure base of self-compassion that will allow you to confidently pursue your valued aims and return occasionally to a safe place that will enable you to rest, to survive, and to thrive, even when your anxiety begs you to turn back. Think of this place as a refuge for your spirit.

When I write about "values," "valued aims," or "valued directions" in this book, I'm using the term "value" to represent behavior that's intrinsically rewarding across time and across situations, as your "heart's deepest desire for how you want to behave in the world."[1]

We all have things specific to us that seem to light a fire beneath us.

So, our values reflect the degree to which certain behaviors are reinforcing, in and of themselves. This, in turn, relates to the consequences of our actions. Let's take a look at a few examples of how values can influence our interactions with our environment and with anxiety:

- Steve, who has great experience and skill with computer technology, doesn't really care about making a lot of money. He values helping people achieve their educational goals. As a result, he refused the offer of a high-pressure, high-paying job that would require long hours and instead has taken on a position that pays less but allows him time to volunteer at a local school to tutor underprivileged children.

- Jane, a mother of two young children, highly values her ability to be a good parent but has an intense fear of social situations. Because of her values, however, she's willing to face her fear, and she agrees to meet up with other parents in her neighborhood so that her children might have playdates and make more friends.

- Jacob is a talented artist who has been accepted to a sculpting course that will help develop his skills and possibly lead to commissions. The studio is in the heart of the city, and his only viable means of getting there on time each day is the subway, but he's afraid of traveling in confined spaces. Yet because he values both his work and the teaching the course provides, he has been able to confront his fears, even though it has been very difficult. He copes with his anxiety by focusing on his aim (the completion of the course), even when he sometimes experiences panic attacks en route.

Research has demonstrated that when people engage more fully in behaviors that give them a sense of pleasure and mastery, they can begin to overcome negative emotions. In fact, these kinds of behaviors may be more effective in overcoming negative emotions than psychiatric medication or than some therapeutic treatments for depression.[2] Research has also indicated that what most effectively changes our negative thinking is engaging in behaviors that help us move in the direction of our valued aims[3] and that by doing so, even in the presence of distress, we can also help ourselves overcome our problems with anxiety.[4] So, in order to engage in truly compassionate behavior and take good care of ourselves, it's very helpful for us to move in the direction of our own valued aims.

Let's take a moment now to discover what valued aims and directions are meaningful and worthwhile to you. What are you willing to experience anxiety and fear in the service of? What behaviors are intrinsically rewarding to you? If you were to be compassionate toward yourself and courageous in your pursuit of your valued aims, where would you be headed? The following worksheet will help you be the author of your own valued directions and begin to pursue your valued aims. Allow yourself the time to complete the worksheet in a place that feels safe to you and where you won't be interrupted. Also schedule another time a day or so later to look at your worksheet and reflect on your answers.

Becoming the Author of My Valued Aims and Directions

This worksheet is intended to give you some space to write down some observations about what valued patterns of behavior you'd like to pursue in your life. Take a few moments to complete each section, and reflect on what aims you might pursue in your life that would be meaningful, be rewarding, and involve a sense of vitality and purpose for you.

1. **Career**

    How important is this area of my life to me? (0–10): _____

    What would my intention be in this area?

    _____

    _____

    _____

    What obstacles might I face in realizing this intention?

    _____

    _____

    _____

    How might I overcome these obstacles?

    _____

    _____

    _____

2. **Family**

    How important is this area of my life to me? (0–10): _____

    What would my intention be in this area?

    _____

    _____

    _____

What obstacles might I face in realizing this intention?

_____

_____

_____

How might I overcome these obstacles?

_____

_____

_____

3.   Intimate Relationships

How important is this area of my life to me? (0–10): _____

What would my intention be in this area?

_____

_____

_____

What obstacles might I face in realizing this intention?

_____

_____

_____

How might I overcome these obstacles?

_____

_____

_____

4. **Social Life**

How important is this area of my life to me? (0–10): _____

What would my intention be in this area?

_____

_____

_____

What obstacles might I face in realizing this intention?

_____

_____

_____

How might I overcome these obstacles?

_____

_____

_____

5. **Education**

How important is this area of my life to me? (0–10): _____

What would my intention be in this area?

_____

_____

What obstacles might I face in realizing this intention?

_____

_____

_____

How might I overcome these obstacles?

_____

_____

_____

6. Physical Well-Being

How important is this area of my life to me? (0–10): _____

What would my intention be in this area?

_____

_____

_____

What obstacles might I face in realizing this intention?

_____

_____

_____

How might I overcome these obstacles?

_____

_____

_____

7. Spirituality

How important is this area of my life to me? (0–10): _____

What would my intention be in this area?

_____

_____

_____

What obstacles might I face in realizing this intention?

_____

_____

_____

How might I overcome these obstacles?

_____

_____

_____

8. **Community Involvement**

How important is this area of my life to me? (0–10): _____

What would my intention be in this area?

_____

_____

_____

What obstacles might I face in realizing this intention?

_____

_____

_____

How might I overcome these obstacles?

_____

_____

_____

9. **Hobbies and Recreation**

How important is this area of my life to me? (0–10): _____

What would my intention be in this area?

_____

_____

_____

What obstacles might I face in realizing this intention?

_____

_____

_____

How might I overcome these obstacles?

_____

_____

_____

REFLECTING ON YOUR VALUED AIMS AND PLANNING FOR COMPASSIONATE BEHAVIOR

After you've completed the worksheet and can take some time to reflect on what you've learned, remember that a short exercise in a book like this isn't necessarily going to become the blueprint for a whole new life; however, it can be one step toward your gradual process of developing compassionate behavior and mindfulness. When your behavior becomes consistent with what you value, you're closer to living a life of compassion and on the way to being better able to face and overcome your fear and anxiety in the service of a life well lived. This might mean making some difficult decisions. For example, if you value physical well-being you may need to refrain from eating foods that taste good but could pose a health risk to you. You might desire an extra glass of wine or two, but you might begin to forgo that kind of indulgence so that you might live a healthier and more productive life. Each of us is unique, with a different set of values, different physical and emotional strengths, and a different learning history; however, we all have the capacity to cultivate our compassionate and mindful emotion-regulation system and to develop our compassionate selves through the many skills and attributes of our compassionate minds. An important part of that process is to face our fears in order to move toward what matters most to us.

DEVELOPING THE MOTIVATION TO FACE YOUR FEARS

In this next section we'll look at the outline of a systematic plan for gradually facing your anxiety and for gradually exposing you to the experiences you'd much rather avoid. In order to prepare for this, it's useful to enhance your compassionate motivation.

There are many reasons we may experience problems with anxiety in our lives. Sometimes, our experience of anxiety seems clearly related to an ongoing psychological problem or anxiety disorder and may include such compulsions as repeatedly checking the oven to see whether the gas has been switched off. At other times, stressful events in our lives, such as unemployment, the breakup of a relationship, or some other loss, may increase our experience of anxiety. From the perspective of the compassionate mind, it's important to remember that the anxiety you experience is *not your fault*—you didn't choose to have such an active threat-detection system or the many reasons and causes for your struggle with anxiety. As much as you can, aim to have compassion for yourself and acceptance of your anxiety, knowing that your suffering is a fundamental part of being human. Recognizing that this is a part of your essential humanity, and having sensitivity to that, may help increase your motivation to face your fears and move toward the life you wish to live.

A life ruled by anxiety is filled with missed opportunities and experiences. When you have some uninterrupted time in your safe place, take a moment to recognize and reflect on what you may have sacrificed or be missing out on because of anxiety. Jot down your answers to the following questions:

- How much has your struggle with anxiety cost you in terms of your personal relationships? Have you avoided relationships, or have they become strained due to the limits your anxiety has placed on you?

- Have you avoided things because of your anxiety and as a result missed out on financial, career, or social opportunities? Have you made decisions that have had a negative impact on your work life or your financial life that have been based in anxiety?

- Has your struggle with anxiety limited the amount of freedom you have to pursue the things that you enjoy? Have you given up recreational activities, travel, or hobbies due to avoidance behaviors?

- How much time and energy have you spent absorbed in negative emotions involved with your struggle with anxiety?

- What other things have you given up due to anxiety? What has anxiety cost you overall in your life?

As you answer these questions, it's likely that you'll begin to understand the impact that your anxiety has had on your life. The good news is that you're now taking steps to overcome this anxiety and to take your life back.

As we near the gradual exposure exercise in this chapter, it's important to remember your aim to reclaim your life and to free yourself to experience life with kindness, courage, and authority. In engaging in exposure, you're going to be willingly experiencing some anxiety and distress in the short term so that you might better overcome anxiety in the long term.

Engaging in compassionate gradual exposure asks us to accept the fact that we may feel more anxiety before we feel less. By now you know that anxiety can arrive suddenly and move through us to activate our physical sensations, emotions, and thoughts. You also know that anxiety isn't easily controlled or suppressed and that the key is to meet it with compassionate courage and tolerate the distress. In CFT we often use the motto "challenging but not overwhelming" to describe this gradual way of approaching anxiety.

With this in mind, use the chart set out below to record and examine the costs and benefits of engaging in compassionate gradual exposure. Imagine for a moment that I had a great fear of public speaking but a willingness to speak in public would be beneficial to my work as a psychologist, not only because of the need to lecture at my university but also to give workshops and discuss research with groups of colleagues. So, if I had a phobia of public speaking it'd probably be a good idea for me to aim to overcome it. If I were to look at the costs and benefits of engaging in gradual exposure to this fear, I would probably list a number of costs. First, engaging in the exposure would cause me to feel anxious, both at the time of exposure and in anticipation of it. If I were engaging in this with the help of a therapist, I may also have to consider the cost of the therapy sessions and the cost in terms of time and effort. On the other hand, if I were to think about the benefits of engaging in gradual exposure, I'd realize that if I overcame my anxiety and fears I'd no longer be inclined to avoid situations where I'd be required to speak in public. Additionally, this exposure might help me reduce my anxiety in a wide range of other situations over the course of my career and possibly make new opportunities available to me, such as speaking at conferences and learning more from my colleagues, whom I would be able to speak with more freely. So, even though there might have been some well-defined costs, I can see how the benefits of engaging in this method of treatment would clearly outweigh them and that the act of engagement would be an exercise in compassion and courage.

In the table below, list the specific costs and benefits that you might face:

Costs of Facing My Fears	Benefits of Facing My Fears

What have you discovered after listing and reviewing the costs and benefits of gradual exposure? Have you created a clear vision of how your life would be improved by coping with your anxiety? You might want to review the list you made in chapter 5 to describe the ways that your life would be improved by your ability to cope with anxiety in a more mindful and compassionate way.

EXPOSURE ON A GRADUAL, COMPASSIONATE PATH

Compassionate gradual and systematic progress through a hierarchy of challenging experiences can help you overcome anxiety.

Exposure is a method of therapy that has been used for decades to help people overcome their fears by guiding them to remain in the presence of situations that cause them to experience elevated levels of anxiety. When we willingly remain close to what causes us fear, gradually fear can lose its power over our behavior. How does this work?

Well, from a certain point of view, exposure works through a process known as habituation. For a very long time, behavior therapists have understood that when we remain in the presence of anxiety-provoking things for long enough, gradually our capacity to remain frightened in a given situation becomes exhausted. What tends to happen with people with anxiety is that they miss out on habituation: rather than staying with the situation until their anxiety begins to go away, they leave the situation while their anxiety is still building or intense. Or, because the thought of such a situation makes them anxious, they avoid it altogether. But, as you've learned, this *can actually make things worse*. The reason is that when people briefly encounter an anxiety-provoking situation and then run away from it, they never learn that their anxiety would eventually subside to a manageable level; thus they're unlikely ever to be less frightened of the situation. This is why it's important to experience through compassionate mindfulness that anxiety doesn't exist as a permanent, endless state of affairs.

It may help to measure your own anxiety by grading it on a scale from 0 to 10, where 0 represents no anxiety at all and 10 the highest anxiety you could ever feel. This mindful process is sometimes referred to as a rating of Subjective Units of Distress, or SUD. Therapists often introduce anxiety-provoking images into their sessions as part of the process of gradually engaging in exposure; for example, if you have a fear of dogs, your therapist might show you pictures of dogs. The therapist would then ask you what your SUD rating would be as you looked at a picture, which you'd continue to do until your anxiety peaked and then until your feelings of anxiety reduced by half. The two of you would decide how to gradually introduce more and more anxiety-provoking things into the situation week by week. For example, after looking at pictures of dogs, you might watch a video of dogs, then visit a pet store to see a dog in a cage. Gradually your exposure might involve approaching a dog, petting a puppy, or even playing with a fully grown Doberman. The speed of the procress would depend on how much your anxiety decreased according to your SUD.

Similar to habituation is desensitization, which results when you use your imagination to engage in and gradually decrease your experience of fear, panic, and anxiety, a process known as imaginary exposure (as opposed to real-life exposure). When you practice imaginary exposure, however, something else is going on beyond the exhaustion of your ability to feel anxious. For one thing, you learn to be less frightened of being frightened; less anxious about being anxious. You begin to see that there are always going to be things that will make you anxious, such as taking exams, major surgery (either for ourselves or for someone we care for), or the need to find a new job. If you're able to tolerate your anxiety-related distress and accept that anxiety is a part of life, then you'll also be able to work with it and around it—in short, you'll be better able to function in your life.

In addition, it seems that when we remain in the presence of an anxiety-provoking situation long enough, we have an opportunity to learn a range of new behaviors in response to that situation instead of just the "fight, flight, or freeze" mode of operating. A practice of mindful and compassionate attention helps us to do this by giving us courage to face our fears. Remember, we learn to swim by being in the water; it's not enough to read the manual on how to do the backstroke.

The program I've outlined below is based on years of research and development in CBT and CFT and can help you begin to work with exposure on your own—again, not just by reading through the steps but also by putting them into practice. Take these exercises only as far as feels right to you, and explore the possibility of working with a support group for anxiety. Additionally, I highly recommend that you seek out a qualified CFT or CBT therapist to help you along the way.

Step One: What Triggers Your Fear?

When you engage in gradual exposure, the experience will depend on the focus of your fear (e.g., fear of flying, fear of dogs, fear of being in enclosed spaces) and the form of your avoidance behavior (e.g., your "fight, flight, or freeze" response).

To begin, it's important to identify and note down what your fears are, and what situations trigger elevated levels of anxiety for you. As you begin to think about your fears, include the range of different situations and experiences in the outside world, and in your mind, that may trigger your threat-detection system.

To prepare, find a time when you can sit in your safe place without interruption for a while. Assume a grounded and stable seated posture, as you do when you're practicing mindfulness and compassionate imagery exercises. Start by taking a few soothing-rhythm breaths, emphasizing the exhale and then slowing the breathing down. Remind yourself that experiencing anxiety is a natural part of life, that it can be challenging, and that your fears and worries are not your fault. Recognize that as you begin to list your fears in preparation for gradual exposure, you're engaging in a courageous and compassionate behavior and moving toward taking care of yourself as best as you can. These steps are meant to be challenging but not overwhelming.

When you're ready, use the form below to list the events "outside" yourself—the situations, events, people, and things—that provoke problematic levels of anxiety for you. Feel free to list whatever comes to mind in this area and in whatever order. Let's look at an example of some of the situations that Jennifer, the client I introduced earlier, would have written down in such a list. Jennifer experienced panic attacks, had some social anxiety, and had some persistent worries about approval and work performance. When her therapy with me began, panic attacks were on the top of her list, and her list of feared situations read something like this:

Jennifer's Anxiety-Provoking and Feared Situations and Circumstances

Riding on the subway

Speaking in front of class

Driving over the George Washington Bridge

Being in closed spaces

Meeting new people

Being in a crowded room

Your list may be very different, because it will be unique to you. You might notice that just thinking about some of these things and writing them down can be a little anxiety provoking. This is another example of how your always-on, "better safe than sorry" threat-detection system is ready to fire up at a moment's notice in order to keep you safe. Take a moment, though, to realize that this is completely natural, and bring yourself back into the present, connecting with the rhythm of your breathing and holding yourself in kindness.

My Anxiety-Provoking and Feared Situations and Circumstances

The next list will involve those "inside" events—the mental events, thoughts, images, and physical sensations—that provoke anxiety and lead you into states of fear and worry. Many of these may seem to pop into your head all on their own or make you feel physically anxious without any prior warning, which in itself can provoke a great deal of anxiety. Just as we did with the list of "outside" events, let's take a look at a few of the thoughts, emotions, and images that Jennifer listed as she began her program of gradual exposure:

Jennifer's Anxiety-Provoking Thoughts and Feared Inner Experiences

"I'm going to freak out."

"I can't handle it in here."

"I think I'm going to have a heart attack."

"I'm going to faint."

"I can't escape!"

"I'm going to freeze up in front of the class."

Picturing myself passed out on the floor of the train

Imagining myself being fired for not being able to speak in front of the class

Feeling nauseous

Feeling dizzy

Feeling "closed in"

We can see a range of different anxiety-provoking thoughts that made their way onto Jennifer's list, as well as the physical sensations related to panic attacks, and images that Jennifer identified as her "inside" experiences that triggered her fear and anxiety. Now it's your turn again; use the form below to record your anxiety-provoking thoughts, sensations, and inner experiences:

My Anxiety-Provoking Thoughts and Feared Inner Experiences

Many people describe how writing down their thoughts helps give them distance from and perspective on their anxiety-provoking thoughts and inner dialogue. You might recall from the section on compassionate thinking that distancing yourself from and observing your anxiety-provoking and distressing mental events is an important step in developing a new and self-compassionate response system. This exercise is aimed at giving you similar distance so that you can observe your mental events with more flexibility, mindfulness, and compassionate awareness and, in turn, move forward to develop a way to cope with your anxious suffering.

Step Two: What Are Your Safety and Avoidance Behaviors?

As discussed in chapter 2, we've evolved to respond to perceived threats with an experience of anxiety and with avoidance behavior. Understandably, avoiding real dangers in the outside world can be a lifesaving strategy; however, it seems that problems arise when safety behaviors and avoidance strategies are used in response to our internal experiences of anxiety. Safety behaviors sometimes have unintended consequences, which may include a rise in anxiety-related behavior in the long run and missing out on valuable experiences in the present moment of our day-to-day lives. Safety behaviors are activated by our "better safe than sorry" threat-detection system and help us only in the short term; so, how do we devise a strategy that can help us in the long term?

There's a substantial and compelling base of research that shows how efforts at suppressing distressing thoughts and avoiding emotional experiences can actually lead to an increase in the very thoughts and feelings we're attempting to suppress.[5] I've seen this for myself when I've worked with clients who've struggled with their anxiety, and I've seen it in my own experience of anxiety. The old adage that "what we resist persists" really does seem to hold true. However, we can develop our compassionate minds to help us overcome our tendency toward unhealthy avoidance and give us courage to face what we fear. Think about it this way: A six-year-old boy becomes anxious at the prospect of going to a friend's birthday party. At this party will be many of his classmates, but also many children he won't know. His mother doesn't like to see him anxious and so tells him, "Don't worry—you don't have to go. You can stay home with me." She believes she's done the right thing to alleviate his distress; unfortunately, what the boy learns is that anxiety is too much to face and can be avoided, and that this avoidance has its own reward—staying at home. The gap then widens between his ability to socialize and that of the other children, some of whom have been told that they're going to the party regardless of their anxiety but that they'll be okay once they get there: "Think of all the cake and the goody bags! And anyway, I'll come get you in only a couple of hours—that's not too long, is it now?" When they go and face the possibility of anxiety, or the initial feelings of anxiety, they're learning to deal with their anxiety and feel it subside as they begin to relax and make friends. Our shy child, on the other hand, feels reassured by being allowed to stay at home, but he's not developing any of the skills needed to make it in the world and cope with his anxiety and develop his confidence. What do you think happens three weeks later when there's another party? Avoidance is not the same as compassion—the shy child's mother wants to be kind, but she's operating in "better safe than sorry" mode; the compassionate mother knows the importance of not doing that, the importance of understanding and validating her child's feelings but also of finding a way to encourage her child.

The CFT approach helps us encourage our own selves with reasoning, kindness, validation of our feelings, and compassion. When we practice imagining the compassionate self, for example, we give the compassionate self a sense of authority, wisdom, and confidence, and it's these qualities that we aim to get in touch with so that we can experience the situations that are difficult for us.

Let's take a look again at Jennifer, whose avoidance and safety behaviors intensified her distress. After having a panic attack on the subway, Jennifer became increasingly convinced that riding certain crowded trains would lead to intolerable levels of anxiety and panic. In response to her fear, she developed a range of safety behaviors she thought would help her avoid an emotional experience that she deemed impossible to bear: she kept one dose of anxiety medication in her purse "in case she needed it" but would never take it; she always carried a full bottle of water on her commute to work "in case she began to feel nauseous"; she took particular books with her on the train so that she could read familiar passages over and over again in order to distract herself; when she could, she'd enlist a "safety person" to ride the train with her; sometimes she took routes that were out of her way just so she could travel on less-crowded trains; additionally, she spent a great deal of money on taxis or walked long distances to stay away from the possibility of having an anxiety attack on the subway.

When she did experience high levels of anxiety or physical sensations that she associated with anxiety and panic, she attempted to suppress these experiences and chided herself for feeling as she did. This resulted in a cycle of intensifying anxiety.

As she and I began working on her compassionate gradual exposure, Jennifer took an inventory of her safety and avoidance behaviors and considered their unintended consequences. After a little while, it became clear that her attempts to ensure control and safety only reinforced her belief that she was in danger and strengthened her cycle of fear and panic. She also realized how much time and effort she was spending to carry out these behaviors—time and effort that could've been devoted to the pursuit of her valued aims and directions.

Just like Jennifer, we all have certain safety behaviors and patterns of avoidance that, despite our intending them for safety, might not be helping us. With this in mind, use the blank form that follows the example below to inventory your own safety behaviors and forms of avoidance.

Jennifer's Safety Behaviors and Forms of Avoidance

Taking taxis rather than riding on the subway

Carrying a bottle of water

Avoiding eye contact when speaking at work

Staying away from crowds

Avoiding bridges

Not attending parties and conferences

Having a "safety person" with me whenever I travel or might become anxious

My Safety Behaviors and Forms of Avoidance

Step Three: Creating Your Fear Hierarchy

A fear hierarchy ranks your feared situations and events in order of how distressing they seem to you. Gradual exposure engagement often uses such a hierarchy as a guide to gradually increase our ability to remain in the presence of difficult experiences. Earlier, you made a list of events and situations in the outside world, and a corresponding list of inner experiences, that you might typically avoid. On the basis of these lists, and anything else that comes to mind, you'll soon create a fear hierarchy of your own that you can use to engage in your own exposure exercises.

On a sheet of paper, list a range of situations and experiences connected to your fears and anxiety. Try to start with the *least* anxiety-provoking circumstance and work your way up to the things you find *most* anxiety provoking. As with the other written exercises, make sure you find a time to do this when you can be in your safe place and when you can do so without interruption.

If you have a fear of flying, your list might include something like "looking at a picture of an airplane" as your least anxiety-provoking circumstance. This might seem rather mild, but remember that even imaginary or pictorial representations of the things that provoke our anxiety can be effective in gradual exposure. If you suffer from claustrophobia-related anxiety, you may list being in an enclosed space from which you can easily exit, such as a phone booth. If you have a fear of having panic attacks in a crowded space, your list may include things like going to a sold-out sporting event or a popular museum exhibit.

You can structure all or part of your list as a sequence of steps; for example, if you have a fear of flying, you might include sitting in an airport terminal, stepping aboard a plane, and remaining aboard for takeoff and flight as separate and progressively anxiety-provoking situations. Be sure that your list includes situations and experiences that provoke a great deal of anxiety, whether or not it seems likely that you'd engage in real-life exposure to them.

Estimate the SUD that you imagine you'd experience during exposure to each of these situations and write it next to each list item. This will help you order the items into a hierarchy using the form below, which you'll use to plan your compassionate gradual exposure. In addition to the SUD, feel free to jot down any observations about how you imagine exposure to this anxiety-provoking situation might affect you.

Below is an example of a completed hierarchy and then a blank form for you to complete yourself.

Jennifer's Fear Hierarchy

Rank	Feared Situation or Experience	SUD 0–10	Observations (optional)
1	Being stuck in a subway car	10	Don't think I could face it!
2	Freezing during a presentation	8	
3	Being humiliated at an office party, saying something stupid	8	Really afraid of the embarrassment
4	Getting stuck on a bridge in a car	7	
5	Feeling crushed in a crowd	6	
6	Going on a first date	6	
7	Meeting people on a job interview	6	
8	Having a panic attack at work	5	I would just feel out of control

My Fear Hierarchy

Rank	Feared Situation or Experience	SUD 0–10	Observations (optional)

Step Four: Prepare to Face Your Feared Situations

The CFT techniques and concepts we've explored will help you prepare for compassionate gradual exposure. It's important to remember that during this process you must remain in the presence of anxiety-provoking circumstances *without blocking or suppressing your anxiety*; however, it's also important to remember that when you practice *compassionate* gradual exposure, you can call on your mindful, compassionate self to give you courage and to hold you in warmth as you face your difficulty. In this way, you're accessing your compassionate emotion-regulation system by being kind to yourself, by being willing, accepting, nonjudgmental, and wise in the knowledge that you're moving toward the pursuit of your valued aims.

As you prepare to engage in compassionate gradual exposure, you may bring to mind the image of your compassionate ideal and remind yourself that—although life is difficult and presents us with many challenges, such as anxiety—anxiety is neither our fault nor our enemy.

Although exposure involves deliberate contact with anxiety, you can remind yourself that over the course of your life, you've encountered anxiety hundreds or thousands of times, sometimes on a daily basis, perhaps so often that it has begun to rule your life. You may often have found yourself engulfed by the activity of your threat-detection system as you acted on autopilot. Now you've begun to understand that you can bring compassion to this realization and deliberately adopt a nonjudgmental acceptance of your experience. In preparation for compassionate gradual exposure, it may be helpful to ask what your compassionate self would say about your engagement in gradual exposure. You may even wish to place your hand or hands over your heart, deliberately directing loving-kindness toward yourself and connecting with a heartfelt desire to alleviate your struggle with anxious suffering.

It may also be helpful for you to visualize what it'd be like to have completed a course of compassionate gradual exposure. What kind of new possibilities would present themselves to you after you learned to cope with and manage your anxiety? Would you feel a sense of accomplishment for calling on your compassionate self to help you have the courage to face your fears?

Find a safe place during a time when you won't be interrupted and where you can sit comfortably, with the soles of your feet on the ground and with your back supported and straight. Begin soothing-rhythm breathing. Let your tongue rest in your jaw, and take a few mindful breaths. With your next natural exhale, begin to follow the steps set out below:

- Create an image of yourself going through the first steps of compassionate gradual exposure.

- Acknowledge that the first steps are likely to be anxiety provoking.

- Bring to mind your compassionate self and imagine that self helping you engage with the anxiety-provoking situation.

- Focus on the feelings that you may have as you compassionately and gradually engage with the situation.

- See yourself coping with the situation, tolerating the anxiety, making contact with your breathing, and using your mindful and compassionate thinking. Focus on the compassionate, validating, and understanding voice that's within you.

- Remind yourself that the anxiety isn't permanent and will ebb just as it flows.

- Walk yourself through the steps you'll be taking, and see yourself coping with them.

- See yourself coming through the anxiety and smiling to yourself with the pleasure of achievement.

This is the ideal situation; however, exposure is a difficult process, and things might not always go according to plan or as you imagined they would. If things get a bit tricky, refer to the following list. (You may find it helpful to write these points on an index card or in your notebook and keep them with you when you practice exposure.)

- Remember that things don't always go smoothly and that you're doing the best you can. It's similar to learning a new sport: sometimes you can see yourself improving, but other times you feel stuck. This is all perfectly normal.

- As much as you can, return to the perspective of your compassionate self and remind yourself you can have another go at this on another day.

- Make sure you haven't tried to engage with something in your hierarchy that is perhaps a bit too much at this stage; alternatively, try to find a way to adapt your exposure to adjust to a possible glitch.

- Always remain self-compassionate when things get difficult. When you hear the voice of your inner critic, acknowledge its presence, but then focus on your breathing and let the criticism go as you refocus on the compassionate gradual exposure.

Step Five: Engaging in Compassionate Gradual Exposure

You've now reached the point where you can begin to engage in compassionate gradual exposure to your anxiety. There are several ways of practicing, but we're going to focus on two methods that are well suited to treating a wide range of anxiety-based problems. The first method is known as imaginary (or imaginal) exposure, which involves imagining that you're in the situation you'd fear. For example, if I were afraid of heights, I might imagine myself standing on a high floor of a skyscraper and peering down at the streets dizzyingly far below. Although this isn't as anxiety provoking as the real thing, it still makes my body and mind respond as if it were happening in real life. Therefore, imaginary exposure is an effective method of introduction to compassionate gradual exposure.

The second method you'll be practicing is known as real-life exposure, in which you actually face and engage with the situations and circumstances you've listed in your fear hierarchy. You won't be putting yourself in situations that could cause you harm, but you will be willingly entering into situations that cause you anxiety. So, if I were engaging in real-life exposure with my fear of heights, I'd purchase a ticket to the eighty-sixth floor of the Empire State Building, ride the elevator up, and actually stand on that observation deck rather than just imagining that I'm doing so. As you might expect, truly facing the things that frighten you through real-life exposure can be challenging, but it can also be a highly effective way to liberate yourself from your fears.

As you move up the fear hierarchy, you're likely to experience greater levels of anxiety, but this is part of the process of overcoming anxiety through compassionate gradual exposure, and as you engage in the exercise it's important that you recognize and let go of any safety or avoidance behaviors. As you've seen, these behaviors typically help you only in the short term; in the long term, they prevent you from pursuing your valued aims and directions. Letting go of these behaviors to fully engage with the process of exposure is a mindful act of courage and self-compassion.

Imaginary Exposure

Find a time and a place where you can sit quietly without interruption and with your eyes closed for about ten to fifteen minutes. Based on the situations you listed in your fear hierarchy, you're going to imagine scenarios in which you encounter your fears. This first time, you'll begin with the situation that provokes the least anxiety.

Begin with your soothing-rhythm breathing—the soles of your feet are grounded, your posture is straight, you're comfortable and supported, and you've allowed the hint of a smile to form. Your eyes remain closed, but you're alert. After a few moments, begin to imagine the scenario that corresponds to the bottom item on your hierarchy, as vividly as you can. Stay with this imaginary situation as if it were actually happening in the present moment. You may begin to feel some anxiety, but it's important to resist the temptation to engage in any safety or avoidance behaviors. You're learning to willingly stay with the image that frightens you. Every two minutes or so, rate your SUD on a scale from 0 to 10. This will help you notice your distress level off and decrease.

Continue to imagine the situation until you believe you've habituated to it, a sensation that may even be indicated by feelings of boredom. In fact, if you start to feel bored, that's great! Isn't boredom preferable to the anxiety or fear you previously related to the situation? As you become less anxious, your attention can turn itself to other things and, by doing so, give you the opportunity to respond in new ways to things you previously felt anxious about. You're learning that you can face your fear and that you don't need to heed your threat-detection system when it sets off false alarms. Once you feel ready, move on to the next item in your hierarchy.

Do this for ten to fifteen minutes, or until your SUD rating reaches a peak of 10 and then drops to about half of that. This drop in SUD represents habituation, which will help you become familiar with the feeling of anxiety and then also with relief once your anxiety begins to subside. The more often you experience the rise and fall of anxiety in an imaginary situation, the less anxiety-provoking this situation will be in the long term.

You should aim to practice this exercise daily, gradually working your way up your hierarchy until you reach the top—until you feel familiar with, or habituated to, the feeling of anxiety and the corresponding feeling of relief as the anxiety dissipates when you imagine that situation.

As you practice compassionate gradual exposure, it's a good idea to contact your compassionate self after each session. Throughout, you should stay with your stable posture, a kind half-smile, closed eyes, and soothing-rhythm breathing.

Drop into the present moment with the next natural inhale and bring the image of your compassionate self to mind. For a few moments, imagine what your compassionate self would say about your engagement with compassionate gradual exposure. Give yourself credit and appreciation for having the courage to turn toward those things that cause you fear in order to live your life more fully and follow in the direction of your valued aims.

It's important to engage in compassionate gradual exposure voluntarily and at a pace that feels right to you. The process should be challenging but not overwhelming, not so difficult that it makes you distraught, discouraged, and ready to give up trying. Remember to be kind to yourself, even as you face your fears.

You can record your progress in compassionate gradual imaginary exposure using the chart below, noting any observations that you wish to remember along the way. The example uses the top item from Jennifer's fear hierarchy.

Jennifer's Imaginary Exposure Record

Date: August 12, 2012		
Feared Situation: Being stuck for hours in a subway car without air conditioning		
Time	SUD (0–10)	Observations (optional)
Start: 1:58	8	This seems like it could be bad.
2:00	9	
2:03	10	Very anxious now.
2:06	10	Why am I doing this?
2:08	8	
2:10	7	Okay, this is easing up a bit.
2:12	6	
2:15	5	Getting used to it.

My Imaginary Exposure Record

Date:		
Feared Situation:		
Time	**SUD (0–10)**	**Observations (optional)**
Start:		

REAL-LIFE EXPOSURE

After some time spent practicing, you may find that imaginary exposure has helped you begin to reduce the level of anxiety you experience when you think about the situations and events in your fear hierarchy. This is good news and represents progress. From here you may begin to engage in real-life exposure, the second method of compassionate gradual exposure. This follows a format similar to that of the imaginary method, but this time you'll be facing anxiety-provoking situations in the real world rather than in your imagination. It's important to recognize that you're not being asked to face situations that put you at risk of physical harm. The aim here is for you to bring yourself into contact with situations that trigger intense levels of anxiety and fear, not to face dangerous situations.

Just as with imaginary exposure, while you're undergoing this exercise it may help you to record your SUD rating every two minutes. Stay with the exposure until your SUD rating peaks and then drops by half. Again, it's important to proceed gradually and to be sensitive to your own limits. I like to tell my clients that they can work on the edge of their comfort zone, gradually stretching their capacity to tolerate distress and anxiety step by step. This can be a bit trickier with real-life exposure than it is with imaginary exposure, since real-life situations can't always be kept to brief or limited periods. For example, if I'm afraid of flying and am engaging in real-life exposure to a short commercial flight, the most anxiety-provoking situation on my fear hierarchy, I obviously won't be able to do that for only ten or fifteen minutes as I did with my imaginary method. So, you need to be sensitive to this, creative in your approach to practicing real-life exposure, and willing and prepared to face life on its own terms. Working with your compassionate mind and accessing your compassionate self can be very helpful in these situations, when they can give you the courage to face your anxiety and follow your valued aims and directions.

Additionally, many of my CFT clients have found it useful to create a series of "coping statements," based on compassionate thinking, before entering into anxiety-provoking situations, such as in real-life exposure. These statements have traditionally been written on postcards of my clients' choosing, which we've called coping cards. Recently, an increasing number of my clients have preferred to record these notes in an app on their mobile phones. In order to come up with some of these statements, you might ask yourself what you'd like to hear from a loving, strong, and supportive friend who was walking alongside you as you engaged in your compassionate gradual exposure. What words of encouragement, support, and authoritative helpfulness would help you to feel safe, resilient, and ready to move forward in the face of fear, difficult emotions, and anxiety? Below are a few examples of compassionate coping statements that may be helpful. Feel free to use these yourself, but try also to come up with your own statements that are uniquely suitable to you:

- *Anxiety is a natural part of life, and it makes sense that I'd feel this way.*

- *I know these anxious feelings are unpleasant, but I also know that I'm not in any danger. I can tell that these uncomfortable emotions and sensations are anxiety, because they've been triggered by these predictable circumstances that I've begun to engage in.*

- *If this were a problem more serious than anxiety, then it wouldn't come and go as it does.*

Close your eyes for a moment and think about these statements, slowly breathing in and out. Bring to mind the sense of being a compassionate person and the image of your compassionate self, complete with a sense of wisdom and a genuine wish to be helpful, caring, and warm. Now, open your eyes and read those statements again, but this time focus on their kindness and understanding. Don't worry about whether you believe them or not, or whether they're accurate or not; just focus on your emotions as you speak the words out loud.

Did you notice any difference? Here are some further coping statements to help you work from a compassionate, feeling perspective:

- *Experiencing anxiety is not my fault; it's just a part of being human.*

- *Feelings are not facts.*

- *Emotions and responses like anxiety are not permanent; they will pass.*

- *This feeling will rise and fall, and I can ride it like a wave until it dissipates.*

- *By facing this fear, I'm opening myself up to living more fully and in the direction of my valued aims.*

So, by willingly engaging in compassionate gradual exposure to real-life situations that make you anxious, and by responding to your anxiety with compassion, courage, and wisdom, you're taking strong steps in compassionate behavior that can lead you from a life dominated by anxiety to a life directed toward valued aims. The form that follows will help you keep track of your progress.

My Real-Life Exposure Record

Date:		
Feared Situation:		
Time	**SUD (0–10)**	**Observations (optional)**
Start:		

TAKING COMPASSIONATE EXPOSURE FURTHER AND FACING FEAR IN EVERYDAY LIFE

The plan for gradual exposure that we've worked through is a structured way to face anxiety and overcome the hold anxiety has on your behavior and your life; however, the ultimate aim is for you to use the lessons of compassionate gradual exposure in your everyday behavior. A good way to practice this is by performing a behavioral experiment: notice the anxiety-provoking situations you might have to engage with; then, when you do engage, observe your anxiety response and carry on to complete your engagement with the situation.

Let's look at some examples of behavioral experiments in action. If I were a chronic worrier and heading out to the south of Spain for a holiday, my mind might generate a host of anxious predictions. I might pester myself with "what ifs," such as *What if I get stuck in traffic and miss my flight?* and *What if I get food poisoning?*; however, if I engaged in behavioral experiments, I would notice my anxious prediction that I could get stuck in traffic, pause to validate and understand that prediction, and then use compassionate attention to refocus my thoughts on the happy times I'll have on the vacation I have planned. After arriving at the airport, I might look back on my worrisome predictions and see how accurate they may have been, given that I left the house late and there was an accident en route. I might also notice that I was able to cope with the possibility of the delay by realizing that I hadn't left the house that late, that the accident was out of my control (and hope that no one was badly injured), and that my anxiety was not my fault. Regardless, so much of our suffering due to anxiety is due to worrisome predictions about things that never come to pass. Often, when things do go wrong, we have far greater coping resources than we're led to believe by our anxious minds, given that they're focused on our worry instead of on the big picture. By cultivating your compassionate mind, you can engage in these behavioral experiments as often as seems workable while bringing mindful, compassionate behavior; wisdom; and courage into your everyday life.

10

Moving Forward with Compassion and "Beginning Again, Constantly"

Having compassion starts and ends with having compassion for all those unwanted parts of ourselves, all those imperfections that we don't even want to look at. Compassion isn't some kind of self-improvement project or ideal that we're trying to live up to.

—Pema Chödrön, *When Things Fall Apart*

My own study and practice of psychology, compassionate mind training, and mindfulness has been a deeply personal journey, as well as a professional mission.

We all share a common fate in our shared suffering, and my own unfolding history of loss, fear, and trauma has taught me a great deal about what it means to approach my experience of anxiety with as much self-kindness, willingness, and courage as I can, moment by moment. This isn't a process that reaches a point of completion. Every day there are new challenges, new worries, and new encounters with emotional pain and doubt. Each moment presents an opportunity to return to a compassionate perspective, no matter how distressed we are. The English guitarist and expert on contemplative practice Robert Fripp has said, "We begin again constantly." I like this phrase—and remind myself of it when I practice the guitar and when I practice mindfulness and compassionate behavior. It means that in this present moment—the only moment we'll ever really experience—we can choose to make the decision to move forward in the direction of our valued aims—beginning now. This choice is always available to us; it's never too late. We begin again and again, and our evolved capacity for compassion doesn't abandon us. It's available to us as we become available to it.

Ultimately, we all become our own therapists, our own scientists, and our own guides. When I read new research and theories about meditation techniques or psychotherapy methods, I test them for myself as a matter of course. It would mean a great deal to me if you also did this when working with this book. Take *none* of what you've read on faith. Test each method. Explore and validate your own experience. We've looked at a number of ideas and techniques together, and this is the point of departure. Your completion of this book is a beginning, one that will see you engaging with these practices in ways that may help you overcome your struggle with anxiety and move in valued directions.

As you do this, it's important to remember the often-repeated idea that life is not about reaching a destination, but about *the journey*. Your personal path, a life of mindful compassion, *is* your goal, and gently, consistently reminding yourself of this is a very good idea. Developing self-compassion isn't about perfecting yourself or finding a way to reach the top of the mountain; it's about accepting who you are, here and now, in this very moment.

I can clearly remember an evening I spent with warm and wise friends in Boston during the last few weeks of my internship year. I was filled with daydreams, plans, and ambitions about where my life was headed and how good things were going to be when I finally arrived at my destination. My attention and steady stream of chatter were all about how good it was going to be in the future and how much happier I'd be if I became someone new, someone more successful. Meg, one of my friends, took me by the hand for a moment, looked into my eyes, and said, "It's great to hear about all of your plans, Dennis, but I want you to remember that your life is happening right now. This *is* your life. It has already begun, and we are all here together and right now you are already good enough, just as you are, and we love you." This kind of stopped me in my tracks. I felt very moved and filled with gratitude. I'd been so fired up about the possibility for personal transformation and professional development that I couldn't really appreciate the joy and care that was present all around me that night. Of all of the different evenings I've spent with colleagues and buddies, this one often comes to mind. When I think of Meg's words, part of me feels nostalgic for that time in my life, but even that sort of misses the point. Meg was inviting me to show up to my life with compassionate acceptance, in contact with the present moment. Getting pulled into the future or lost in the past is very different from that idea. Right here and right now is where we live our lives. So, as you practice the development of your compassionate mind, my wish for you is that you come into contact with the loving-kindness, courage, warmth, and wisdom that you already possess and that you open yourself up to accepting yourself exactly as you are, in this very moment.

Throughout this book, you've learned that anxiety is a natural part of human experience; that our always-on, "better safe than sorry" threat-detection system has evolved as an essential part of our survival to help our species flourish. You understand that anxiety affects many aspects of us, such as our thoughts, emotions, and physical sensations. You've seen that when our threat-detection system is active and dominant, it uses our "threatened mind" to influence our attention, thinking, motivations, emotions, imagination, and behavior. You understand now that we've evolved to have a powerful capacity to feel fear and to protect ourselves by seeking safety, whether in the company of others or by fleeing a situation altogether. As important as this threat-detection system is, you know that the experience of intense and excessive anxiety can be distressful and can hold us back from fully experiencing our lives.

It's important to remember that our anxious suffering is not our fault. After all, each of us just finds ourselves here, emerging from the evolutionary flow of life on this planet. And, what we think and feel is related to our genetic history and our learning history. You know that we didn't choose to have such tricky brains, but you also know that these allow us to use our learning histories, and the range of our personal circumstances, even traumatic events, to deal with, yet sometimes perpetuate, our troubles with anxiety.

Thankfully, our rapid-response threat-detection system is not our only response system. Our tricky brains have evolved to let us reflect, develop long-term plans, and observe our experiences from a flexible perspective, with wisdom and without judgment. Still more importantly, you've learned that experiencing compassion for ourselves and for others can be one of the most useful tools to help us overcome our difficulties with anxiety, and that kindness, warmth, and a deep sensitivity to suffering in ourselves and others can begin to affect how we cope with our anxiety. CFT is based on the fact that the more we cultivate our capacity for compassion, the more we activate our supportive and positive feelings involving the experience of safety, contentment, and a secure base from which we can explore our world. As these feelings and alternate response systems are strengthened and activated more consistently, we can become more mindful and more in touch with our compassionate selves.

Let's look now at a few ideas and simple steps that can help you continue the cultivation of your compassionate mind in order to overcome your struggle with anxiety. There are many ways that you can approach the material from this book, and the following steps suggest a path that may strengthen your practice and provide you with some structure along the way.

STEPS IN MOVING FORWARD (AND BEGINNING AGAIN, CONSTANTLY!)

1. **Accept that anxious suffering is a part of the human condition.**
    This is a point that we've looked at often, yet I feel that it remains important to outline the steps that you can take to bring compassion to your anxiety. Buddhist nun Pema Chödrön writes, "The first noble truth of the Buddha is that when we feel suffering, it doesn't mean that something is wrong. What a relief. Finally somebody told the truth. Suffering is a part of life, and we don't have to feel it's happening because we personally made the wrong move."[1]

2. **Gradually build your capacity for mindfulness.**

    Mindfulness may not be an end in itself, but it can be an important part of your development of compassion, wisdom, and courage. As you grow in your ability to remain in contact with the present moment, willingly and nonjudgmentally, you may loosen the grip that anxious thoughts and feelings can have on your mind and your behavior. Thousands of years of Eastern meditative tradition as well as advanced Western scientific research have demonstrated how useful mindfulness can be as it helps us overcome our problems with anxiety. The mindfulness exercises in this book can serve as a structure for a daily practice. With consistent, engaged mindfulness practice, your capacity to bring mindfulness to your everyday experience, moment by moment, can grow. You'll develop an important new strength even if you begin by practicing mindfulness for just a few minutes each day. In time, you may build a personal mindfulness practice that involves formal mindfulness training for twenty minutes each day or more. This can greatly benefit your work with anxiety and the development of your compassionate mind. There are links to many resources for continuing your mindfulness practice, as well as several guided mindfulness meditations available for download, on my website, mindfulcompassion.com.

3. **Use compassionate imagery.**

    Your mind's ability to create an imaginary inner world, and to respond to this world with real emotions and behavioral changes, is a powerful tool for your compassionate mind training. Planning to spend some time each day practicing compassionate imagery will help you access self-compassion when you need it. You can practice the longer, structured compassionate imagery exercises, such as Building and Becoming the Compassionate Self or Creating and Encountering the Compassionate Ideal (both in chapter 7), whenever you need to. When you sense feelings of anxiety building up, and may begin to feel overwhelmed, aim to contact the part of you that is supportive, helpful, encouraging, and nonjudgmental. This can help you experience anxiety from a secure base, without being engulfed in the anxiety and feeling completely caught up in your fears.

4. **Return to compassionate thinking.**

When your anxious mind is activated, your attention can become narrower, your range of responses seem limited, and your thinking become threat-focused, worried, and fearful; however, when you activate your compassionate mind you provide yourself with the opportunity to see things from a compassionate perspective and to realize how much of your life you've given up to anxious thinking. When you do this, you can then choose to learn to use your compassionate reasoning to frame new responses that are more in tune with your capacity for warmth, wisdom, and resiliency. The range of compassionate alternative responding techniques I've described are designed to help you practice this and to help you take back control from worry, fear, and panic. The Compassionate-Thought Record (chapter 8) and daily practice of compassionate thinking exercises can help you integrate compassionate responses into your everyday, automatic patterns of reacting to anxiety, and a gradual, step-by-step engagement can help you build a bridge between a life dominated by anxiety and a life in which compassionate action becomes possible.

5. **Set your course, face your fears, and live a life of compassionate behavior.**

We've evolved to seek safety and comfort through affiliation and to find a secure base from which we can explore the world. Affiliation helps us regulate our emotions and, as a result, pursue our valued aims. Similarly, the development of mindful and compassionate attention, compassionate imagery, and compassionate thinking provides a platform of compassionate wisdom that can allow you to build a life worth living. Anxiety can be distressful, but it can also limit your prospects when you avoid certain situations that you fear, engage in hours of worry or compulsive behavior, and spend time and energy engaging in safety behaviors. If you let this happen, anxiety and avoidance can become the organizing principles for how you approach your life. Compassionate behavior involves taking action to identify the way you wish to change this so that you can cope with your anxiety, broaden your perspectives and prospects, clarify your valued aims, and face your fears so that you may live more fulsomely. One of the most compassionate things you can do is become sensitive to suffering and committed to taking action to alleviate that suffering in yourself and others.

Mindful, compassionate gradual exposure to your anxiety is a powerful example of a difficult but worthwhile exercise that can help liberate you from anxiety in the long term. Additionally, as your capacity for compassion grows, you may wish to expand your circle of compassionate behavior by bringing your compassionate self into your life, for example as an active member of your community, as a family member, or as a partner in a personal or working relationship. As your heart opens in warmth and loving-kindness to the common humanity of our anxious struggles, your compassionate attention, thinking, and behavior toward others as well as toward yourself will light the way to your living a bigger, more meaningful life.

"THE GOLDEN RULE": FIRST, INVERSION

As we reach the end of this book about compassion and anxiety, I'd like to acknowledge that there has been a bit of a paradox throughout these pages. We know that anxiety causes us to be fearful of what may happen to *us* and involves a lot of inward focus; compassion, however, usually refers to a focus on others. Compassion is usually referred to in the context of how we're moved by the suffering of others and how we act to help alleviate their suffering. Compassion in this traditional sense is indeed a powerful and important part of contacting your essential humanity and will help you live mindfully and alleviate your own suffering.

In this book I've chosen to focus on how you might develop compassion for yourself and choose to direct your compassionate mind inward so that it can help you cope with your inward-focused anxiety. This choice partly reflects what I refer to as "The Golden Rule: First, Inversion." The Golden Rule, as it is popularly known, means that we should treat others as we'd treat ourselves; however, this assumes that we treat ourselves well and with kindness.[2] I'm afraid that we can't make this assumption. The epidemic levels of anxiety disorders—depression laced with worry—and the general culture of fear and pressure for material success that surrounds us can drag us into a place of shame, self-criticism, and neglect for our own well-being. Perhaps, as my colleague Chris Germer suggested, we need a new Golden Rule, one that directs us to treat ourselves the way we would wish to be treated by others. I like to think of this as an inversion of the Golden Rule, which serves as a reminder of how we might begin again and again to hold ourselves in kindness and access our compassionate selves.

This resonates with the aims of CFT, which teaches that compassion comes from within us but extends to others as we seek to address the suffering that we encounter in the wider world: As Thomas Merton wrote, "The whole idea of compassion is based on a keen awareness of the interdependence of all these living beings, which are all part of one another, and all involved in one another."[3]

I send my warmest wishes to you as you continue on your journey to cultivate your compassionate mind. Please feel free to contact me through my website.

—Namaste.
DT.

Notes

PREFACE

1 Dykas, M. J., & Cassidy, J., "Attachment and the Processing of Social Information across the Life Span: Theory and Evidence," *Psychological Bulletin*, 137(1), (2011), 19–46; Gilbert, P., *The Compassionate Mind: A New Approach to Life's Challenges* (London: Constable & Robinson, 2009).

2 Neff, K. D., Kirkpatrick, K., & Rude, S. S., "Self-compassion and Its Link to Adaptive Psychological Functioning," *Journal of Research in Personality*, 41, (2007), 139–54.

3 Gilbert, P., & Procter, S., "Compassionate Mind Training for People with High Shame and Self-Criticism: A Pilot Study of a Group-Therapy Approach," *Clinical Psychology and Psychotherapy*, 13, (2006), 353–79; Van Dam, N., Sheppard, S. C., Forsyth, J. C., & Earleywine, M., "Self-Compassion Is a Better Predictor than Mindfulness of Symptom Severity and Quality of Life in Mixed Anxiety and Depression," *Journal of Anxiety Disorders*, 25, (2011), 123–30.

A PERSONAL STORY AND ACKNOWLEDGMENTS

1 Hayes, S. C., Strosahl, K. D., & Wilson, K. G., *Acceptance and Commitment Therapy: An Experiential Approach to Behavior Change* (New York: Guilford Press, 2009).

2 Linehan, M. M., *Cognitive Behavioral Treatment of Borderline Personality Disorder* (New York: Guilford Press, 1993).

3 Leahy, R. L., Tirch, D., & Napolitano, L., *Emotion Regulation in Psychotherapy: A Practitioner's Guide* (New York: Guilford Press, 2011).

4 Gilbert, P., McEwan, K., Matos, M., & Rivis, A., "Fears of Compassion: Development of Three Self-Report Measures," *Psychology and Psychotherapy*, (2011) [Epub ahead of print].

5 Gilbert, P., *The Compassionate Mind: A New Approach to Life's Challenges* (London: Constable & Robinson, 2009); Longe, O., Maratos, F. A., Gilbert, P., Evans, G., Volker, F., Rockliff, H., & Rippon, G., "Having a Word with Yourself: Neural Correlates of Self-Criticism and Self-Reassurance," *Neuroimage*, 49(2), (2010), 1849–56.

CHAPTER 1: THE EMERGENCE OF ANXIETY

1 Eysenck, M. W., Derakshan, N., Santos, R., & Calvo, M. G., "Anxiety and Cognitive Performance: Attentional Control Theory," *Emotion*, 7, (2007), 336–53.

2 Hirschfeld, R. M. A., "The Comorbidity of Major Depression and Anxiety Disorders: Recognition and Management in Primary Care," *Primary Care Companion: Journal of Clinical Psychiatry*, 3, (2001), 244–54.

3 Harter, M. C., Conway, K. P., & Merikangas, K. R., "Association between Anxiety Disorders and Physical Illness," *European Archives of Psychiatry and Clinical Neuroscience*, 6, (2003), 313.

4 These statistics, and much more information about anxiety, can be found at adaa.org/about-adaa/press-room/facts-statistics (ADAA, 2011).

5 Kessler, R. C., & Ustun, T. B., *The WHO World Mental Health Surveys* (Cambridge: Cambridge University Press, 2008).

6 Greenberg, P. E., Sisitsky, T., Kessler, R. C., et al., "The Economic Burden of Anxiety Disorders in the 1990s," *Journal of Clinical Psychiatry*, 60, (1999), 427–35.

CHAPTER 2: WHAT IS ANXIETY, AND HOW HAS IT EVOLVED?

1 Hayes, S. C., Strosahl, K. D., & Wilson, K. G., *Acceptance and Commitment Therapy: An Experiential Approach to Behavior Change* (New York: Guilford Press, 1999).

2 A point made by University of Pennsylvania professor A. T. Beck, the founder of cognitive therapy.

3 Adapted from Marks, I. M., & Nesse, R M., "Fear and Fitness: An Evolutionary Analysis of Anxiety Disorders," *Ethology and Sociobiology*, 15 (1994), 247–61.

4 Cook, M., & Mineka, S., "Observational Conditioning of Fear to Fear-Relevant versus Fear-Irrelevant Stimuli in Rhesus Monkeys," *Journal of Abnormal Psychology*, 98 (1989), 448–59.

5 Ferster, C. B., "A Functional Analysis of Depression," *American Psychologist*, 28 (1973), 857–70.

6 Hayes, S. C., Strosahl, K. D., & Wilson, K. G., *Acceptance and Commitment Therapy: An Experiential Approach to Behavior Change* (New York: Guilford Press, 2009).

CHAPTER 3: ANXIETY, COMPASSION, AND OUR ONGOING INTERACTIONS WITH THE WORLD

1 Gilbert, P., *The Compassionate Mind: A New Approach to Life's Challenges* (London: Constable & Robinson, 2009).

2 Goodall, J., *Through a Window: Thirty Years with the Chimpanzees of Gombe* (London: Penguin, 1990).

CHAPTER 4: TOWARD THE COMPASSIONATE MIND: AN EVOLUTION IN OUR UNDERSTANDING OF ANXIETY THROUGH MINDFULNESS, ACCEPTANCE, AND COMPASSION

1 Brownstein, M. J., "A Brief History of Opiates, Opioid Peptides, and Opioid Receptors," *Proceedings of the National Academy of Science*, 90, (1993), 5391–93.

2 Possehl, G., *The Indus Civilization: A Contemporary Perspective* (Lanham, MD: AltaMira Press, 2003).

3 Deikman, A., *The Observing Self: Mysticism and Psychotherapy* (Boston: Beacon Press, 1982).

4 Beck, A. T., *Cognitive Therapy and the Emotional Disorders* (New York: International Universities Press, 1976); Ellis, A., & Dryden, W., *The Practice of Rational Emotive Behavior Therapy* (New York: Springer, 2007).

5 Kabat-Zinn, J., *Full Catastrophe Living* (New York: Delta, 1990).

6 Hayes, S. C., Strosahl, K. D., & Wilson, K. G., *Acceptance and Commitment Therapy: An Experiential Approach to Behavior Change* (New York: Guilford Press, 2009).

7 Hofmann, S. G., Sawyer, A. T., Witt, A. A., & Oh, D., "The Effect of Mindfulness-Based Therapy on Anxiety and Depression: A Meta-analytic Review," *Journal of Consulting and Clinical Psychology*, 78, (2010), 169–83; Baer, R. A., "Mindfulness Training as a Clinical Intervention: A Conceptual and Empirical Review," *Clinical Psychological Science and Practice*, 10, (2003), 125–43.

8 Roemer, L., & Orsillo, S. M., "An Open Trial of an Acceptance-Based Behavior Therapy for Generalized Anxiety Disorder," *Behavior Therapy*, 38, (2007), 78–82; Roemer, L., Orsillo, S. M., & Salters-Pedneault, K., "Efficacy of an Acceptance-Based Behavior Therapy for Generalized Anxiety Disorder: Evaluation in a Randomized Controlled Trial," *Journal of Consulting and Clinical Psychology*, 76, (2008), 1083–89.

9 H. H. Dalai Lama, *Transforming the Mind* (New York: Thorsons, 2000).

10 This quote is from an interview that can be found at http://www.6seconds.org/2007/02/27/the-neural-power-of-leadership-daniel-goleman-on-social-intelligence.

11 Mikulincer, M., & Shaver, P. R., *Attachment in Adulthood: Structure, Dynamics and Change* (New York: Guilford Press, 2007).

12 Gillath, O., Shaver, P. R., & Mikulincer, M., "An Attachment-Theoretical Approach to Compassion and Altruism," in P. Gilbert (ed.), *Compassion: Conceptualisations, Research, and Use in Psychotherapy* (London: Brunner-Routledge, 2005).

13 Uvans-Moberg, K., "Oxytocin May Mediate the Benefits of Positive Social Interaction and Emotions," *Psychoneuroendocrinology*, 23, (1998), 819–35; Kosfeld, M., Heinrichs, M., Zak, P. J., Fischbacher, U., & Fehr, E., "Oxytocin Increases Trust in Humans," *Nature*, 435, (2005), 673–76.

14 Lutz, A., Brefcyznski-Lewis, J., Johnstone, T., & Davidson, R. J., "Regulation of the Neural Circuitry of Emotion by Compassion Meditation: Effects of Meditative Expertise," *Public Library of Science*, 3, (2008), 1–5.

15 LeDoux, J., *The Emotional Brain* (London: Weidenfeld & Nicolson, 1998).

16 LeDoux, J., *The Emotional Brain* (London: Weidenfeld & Nicolson, 1998).

17 Gilbert, P., *The Compassionate Mind: A New Approach to Life's Challenges* (London: Constable & Robinson, 2009); Gilbert, P., McEwan, K., Mitra, R., Franks, L., Richter, A., & Rockliff, H., "Feeling Safe and Content: A Specific Affect Regulation System? Relationship to Depression, Anxiety, Stress and Self-Criticism," *Journal of Positive Psychology*, 3, (2008), 182–91.

18 Panskepp, J., *Affective Neuroscience* (New York: Oxford Press, 1998); Depue, R. A., & Morrone-Strupinsky, J. V., "A Neurobehavioral Model of Affiliative Bonding: Implications for Conceptualizing a Human Trait of Affiliation," *Behavioral and Brain Sciences*, 28, (2005), 313–50.

19 Gilbert, P., *The Compassionate Mind: A New Approach to Life's Challenges* (London: Constable & Robinson, 2009).

20 Wang, S., "A Conceptual Framework for Integrating Research Related to the Physiology of Compassion and the Wisdom of Buddhist Teachings," in P. Gilbert (ed.), *Compassion: Conceptualisations, Research and Use in Psychotherapy* (New York: Routledge, 2005).

21 Armstrong, K., *The Great Transformation: The World in the Time of Buddha, Socrates, Confucius and Jeremiah* (London: Atlantic Books, 2006).

22 Gilbert, P., *The Compassionate Mind: A New Approach to Life's Challenges* (London: Constable & Robinson, 2009).

23 Jung, C. G., "The Archetypes and the Collective Unconscious," in *Collected Works of C. G. Jung*, Vol. 9, Part 1 (New Jersey: Princeton University Press, 1934).

24 Neff, K., *Self-Compassion: Stop Beating Yourself Up and Leave Insecurity Behind* (New York: HarperCollins, 2011); Neff, K. D., Kirkpatrick, K., & Rude, S. S., "Self-Compassion and Its Link to Adaptive Psychological Functioning," *Journal of Research in Personality*, 41, (2007), 139–54.

25 Neff, K., *Self-Compassion: Stop Beating Yourself Up and Leave Insecurity Behind* (New York: HarperCollins, 2011); Neff, K. D., Kirkpatrick, K., & Rude, S. S., "Self-Compassion and Its Link to Adaptive Psychological Functioning," *Journal of Research in Personality*, 41, (2007), 139–54.

26 Seigel, D. J., *The Mindful Brain* (New York: Norton, 2007).

27 Rahula, W., *What the Buddha Taught* (New York: Grove Press, 1959).

28 Lutz, A., Brefcyznski-Lewis, J., Johnstone, T., & Davidson, R. J., "Regulation of the Neural Circuitry of Emotion by Compassion Meditation: Effects of Meditative Expertise," *Public Library of Science*, 3, (2008), 1–5.

29 Chödrön, P., *Start Where You Are: A Guide to Compassionate Living* (Boston: Shambhala, 2003).

CHAPTER 5: THE FIRST TURNING OF THE WHEEL OF COMPASSION: EXPLORING THE ATTRIBUTES AND SKILLS OF THE COMPASSIONATE MIND

1 Leahy, R. L., Tirch, D., & Napolitano, L., *Emotion Regulation in Psychotherapy: A Practitioner's Guide* (New York: Guilford Press, 2011); Tirch, D. D., & Leahy, R. L., "Anxiety and Our Relationship to Emotional Experience: The Role of Emotional Schemas, Psychological Flexibility, and Mindfulness." Paper presented at the International Congress of Cognitive Psychotherapy, Istanbul (June, 2011).

Tirch, D. D., Leahy, R. L., & Silberstein, L. "Relationships among Emotional Schemas, Psychological Flexibility, Dispositional Mindfulness, and Emotion Regulation." Paper presented at the meeting of the Association for Behavioral and Cognitive Therapies, New York (November, 2009).

CHAPTER 6: MINDFULNESS AS A FOUNDATION FOR COMPASSIONATE ATTENTION

1 Watts, A., *The Wisdom of Insecurity* (New York: Vintage, 1968). The British-born Alan Watts was an extremely important philosopher of East/West philosophy, Zen, and Vedanta, writing in the late 1960s and early 1970s. He was a fantastic thinker and recorded some wonderful lectures. I recommend checking him out.

2 Kabat-Zinn, J., *Full Catastrophe Living* (New York: Delta, 1990).

3 Kabat-Zinn, J., Foreword, in F. Didonna (ed.), *Clinical Handbook of Mindfulness* (New York: Springer, 2009); Siegel, R., Germer, C. K., & Olendzki, A., "Mindfulness: What Is It? Where Did It Come From?" in F. Didonna (ed.), *Clinical Handbook of Mindfulness* (New York: Springer, 2009).

4 Wallace, B. A., "A Mindful Balance," *Tricycle*, Spring 60–63 (2008), 109–11.

5 This exercise is adapted from Gilbert, P., *The Compassionate Mind* (London: Constable & Robinson, 2009).

6 Davidson, R. J., Kabat-Zinn, J., Schumacher, J., Rosenkranz, M., Muller, D., et. al., "Alterations in Brain and Immune Function Produced by Mindfulness Meditation," *Psychosomatic Medicine*, 65, (2003), 564–70; Goldin, P. R., & Gross, J. J., "Effects of Mindfulness-Based Stress Reduction (MBSR) on Emotion Regulation in Social Anxiety Disorder," *Emotion*, 10, (2010), 83–91.

7 This exercise has been adapted from multiple sources, including Kabat-Zinn, J., *Wherever You Go, There You Are: Mindfulness Meditation in Everyday Life* (New York: Hyperion, 1994), and Leahy, R. L., Tirch, D., & Napolitano, L., *Emotion Regulation in Psychotherapy: A Practitioner's Guide* (New York: Guilford Press, 2011).

8 This exercise was developed by two pioneers in the application of mindful compassion to psychotherapy, Kristin Neff and Christopher Germer, and appears in Dr. Germer's book *The Mindful Path to Self-Compassion* (New York: Guilford Press, 2009).

9 Adapted from Leahy, Tirch, and Napolitano, *Emotion Regulation in Psychotherapy: A Practitioner's Guide* (New York: Guilford Press, 2011). This exercise was originally adapted from the MBCT protocol, cf., Segal, Z. V., Williams, J. M. G., & Teasdale, J. D., *Mindfulness-Based Cognitive Therapy for Depression: A New Approach to Preventing Relapse* (New York: Guilford Press, 2002).

10 Adapted from Leahy, Tirch, and Napolitano, *Emotion Regulation in Psychotherapy: A Practitioner's Guide* (New York: Guilford, 2011).

11 Kamalashila, *Meditation: The Buddhist Way of Tranquillity and Insight* (Birmingham, England: Windhorst, 1992).

CHAPTER 7: COMPASSION-FOCUSED IMAGERY

1 The compassionate imagery exercises in this chapter have been adapted from CFT exercises found in Gilbert, P., *The Compassionate Mind* (London: Constable & Robinson, 2009), and other, unpublished CFT sources.

CHAPTER 8: COMPASSIONATE THINKING

1 Neff, K., *Self-Compassion: Stop Beating Yourself Up and Leave Insecurity Behind* (New York: HarperCollins, 2011).

2 Gilbert, P., *The Compassionate Mind: A New Approach to Life's Challenges* (London: Constable & Robinson, 2009).

3 Adapted from Hayes, S. C., Strosahl, K. D., & Wilson, K. G., *Acceptance and Commitment Therapy: An Experiential Approach to Behavior Change* (New York: Guilford Press, 1999). Also found in variations in other sources throughout the Association for Contextual Behavioral Science community, cf. contextualpsychology.org.

CHAPTER 9: COMPASSIONATE BEHAVIOR

1 Robb, H. From a personal communication by email (2010).

2 Dimidjian, S., Hollon, S. D., Dobson, K. S., Schmaling, K. B., Kohlenberg, R. J., Addis, M. E., Gallop, R., McGlinchey, J. B., Markley, D. K., Gollan, J. K., Atkins, D. C., Dunner, D. L., & Jacobson, N. S., "Randomized Trial of Behavioral Activation, Cognitive Therapy, and Antidepressant Medication in the Acute Treatment of Adults with Major Depression," *Journal of Consulting and Clinical Psychology*, 74(4), (2006), 658–70.

3 Bennett-Levy, J., "Mechanisms of Change in Cognitive Therapy: The Case of Automatic Thought Records and Behavioural Experiments," *Behavioural and Cognitive Psychotherapy*, 31, (2003), 261–77.

4 Hayes, S. C., Luoma, J., Bond, F., Masuda, A., & Lillis, J., "Acceptance and Commitment Therapy: Model, Processes, and Outcomes," *Behaviour Research and Therapy*, 44(1), (2006), 1–25; Hayes, S. C., from "The Roots of Compassion," a plenary talk at the 2008 conference of the Association for Behavioral and Cognitive Therapies, which can be viewed here: www .globalpres.com/mediasite/Viewer/?peid=017fe6ef4b1544279d8cf27adbe 92a51.

5 Wenzlaff, R. M., & Wegner, D. M., "Thought Suppression," *Annual Review of Psychology*, 51, (2000), 59–91.

CHAPTER 10: MOVING FORWARD WITH COMPASSION AND "BEGINNING AGAIN, CONSTANTLY"

1 Chödrön, P., *When Things Fall Apart* (Boston: Shambhala, 1997).

2 Germer, C., *The Mindful Path to Self-Compassion* (New York: Guilford Press, 2009).

3 Thomas Merton (1915–1968) was a writer and a Trappist monk who encouraged interfaith understanding and was famous for gently integrating Buddhist and Christian philosophy in his work.

Resources

PRINT

Baer, R. A., "Mindfulness Training as a Clinical Intervention: A Conceptual and Empirical Review," *Clinical Psychological Science and Practice*, 10, (2003), 125–43.

Barlow, D., *Anxiety and Its Disorders* (New York: Guilford Press, 2002).

Brach, T., *Radical Acceptance: Embracing Your Life with the Heart of a Buddha* (New York: Bantam, 2004).

Cahn, B. R., & Polich, J., "Meditation States and Traits: EEG, ERP, and Neuroimaging Studies," *Psychological Bulletin*, 132, (2006), 180–211.

Carter, C. S., "Neuroendocrine Perspectives on Social Attachment and Love," *Psychoneuroendocrinology*, 23, (1998), 779–818.

Chödrön, P., *Start Where You Are: How to Accept Yourself and Others* (London: Element/HarperCollins, 2005).

Chödrön, P., *When Things Fall Apart: Heart Advice for Difficult Times* (Boston: Shambhala, 1997).

Cozolino, L., *The Neuroscience of Human Relationships: Attachment and the Developing Brain* (New York: Norton, 2007).

Craske, M. G., Kircanski, K., Zelikowsky, M., Mystkowski, J., Chowdhury, N. & Baker, A., "Optimizing Inhibitory Learning During Exposure Therapy," *Behavior Research Therapy*, 46, (2008), 5–27.

Dalai Lama, *An Open Heart: Practicing Compassion in Everyday Life* (New York: Little, Brown, 2001).

Dalai Lama, *The Power of Compassion* (India: HarperCollins, 1995).

Dalai Lama & Cutler, H., *The Art of Happiness: A Handbook for Living* (New York: Riverhead Books, 1998).

Dalai Lama & Ekman, P., *Emotional Awareness: Overcoming the Obstacles to Psychological Balance and Compassion* (New York: Henry Holt, 2008).

Davidson, R., & Harrington, A. *Visions of Compassion: Western Scientists and Tibetan Buddhists Examine Human Nature* (Oxford: Oxford University Press, 2002).

Depue, R. A., & Morrone-Strupinsky, J. V., "A Neurobehavioral Model of Affiliative Bonding: Implications for Conceptualizing a Human Trait of Affiliation," *Behavioral and Brain Sciences*, 28, (2005), 313–50.

Farb, N. A. S., Segal, Z., Mayberg, V., Bean, H. J., McKeon, D., Fatima, Z., et al., "Attending to the Present: Mindfulness Meditation Reveals Distinct Neural Modes of Self-Reference," *Social Cognitive Affective Neuroscience Advance Access*, 2, (2007), 1–10.

Germer, C. K., *The Mindful Path to Self-Compassion: Freeing Yourself from Destructive Thoughts and Emotions* (New York: Guilford Press, 2009).

Gilbert, P., *The Compassionate Mind* (London: Constable & Robinson, 2009).

Gilbert, P., *Compassion Focused Therapy: Distinctive Features* (London: Routledge, 2010).

Gilbert, P., *Human Nature and Suffering* (London: Lawrence Erlbaum Associates, 1989).

Gilbert, P., McEwan, K., Mitra, R., Franks, L., Richter, A., & Rockliff, H., "Feeling Safe and Content: A Specific Affect Regulation System? Relationship to Depression, Anxiety, Stress, and Self Criticism," *Journal of Positive Psychology*, 3, (2008), 182–91.

Hanson, R., & Mendius, R., *Buddha's Brain: The Practical Neuroscience of Happiness, Love, and Wisdom* (Oakland, CA: New Harbinger, 2009).

Hayes, S. C., Luoma, J., Bond, F., Masuda, A., & Lillis, J., "Acceptance and Commitment Therapy: Model, Processes, and Outcomes," *Behaviour Research and Therapy*, 44(1), (2006), 1–25.

Henderson, L., *Improving Social Confidence and Reducing Shyness Using Compassion Focused Therapy* (London: Constable & Robinson, 2010).

Hofmann, S. G., Sawyer, A. T., Witt, A. A., & Oh, D., "The Effect of Mindfulness-Based Therapy on Anxiety and Depression: A Meta-Analytic Review," *Journal of Consulting and Clinical Psychology*, 78, (2010), 169–83.

Jung, C. G., "The Archetypes and the Collective Unconscious," in *Collected Works of C. G. Jung* Vol. 9, Part 1 (New Jersey: Princeton University Press, 1934).

Kabat-Zinn, J., *Coming to Our Senses: Healing Ourselves and the World through Mindfulness* (New York: Piatkus, 2005).

Kabat-Zinn, J., *Wherever You Go, There You Are: Mindfulness Meditation in Everyday Life* (New York: Hyperion, 1994).

Kornfield, J., *A Path with Heart* (New York: Bantam Books, 1993).

Kritikos, P. G., & Papadaki, S. P., "The Early History of the Poppy and Opium," *Journal of the Archaeological Society of Athens*, (1967).

Lazar, S. W., Kerr, C. E., Wasserman, R. H., Gray, J. R., Greve, D. N., Treadway, M. T., et al., "Meditation Experience Is Associated with Increased Cortical Thickness," *Neuroreport*, 16(17), (2005), 1893–97.

Leahy, R. L., *Anxiety Free* (New York: Hay House, 2010).

Linehan, M. M., *Cognitive Behavioral Treatment of Borderline Personality Disorder* (New York: Guilford Press, 1993).

Longe, O., Maratos, F. A., Gilbert, P., Evans, G., Volker, F., Rockliff, H., & Rippon, G., "Having a Word with Yourself: Neural Correlates of Self-Criticism and Self-Reassurance," *Neuroimage*, 49(2), (2010), 1849–56.

Lutz, A., Brefcyznski-Lewis, J., Johnstone, T., & Davidson, R. J., "Regulation of the Neural Circuitry of Emotion by Compassion Meditation: Effects of Meditative Expertise," *Public Library of Science*, 3, (2008), 1–5.

Mikulincer, M., & Shaver, P. R., *Attachment in Adulthood: Structure, Dynamics, and Change* (New York: Guilford Press, 2007).

Mingyur Rinpoche, Y., *The Joy of Living: Unlocking the Secret and Science of Happiness* (New York: Harmony Books, 2007).

Neff, K. D., *Self-Compassion: Stop Beating Yourself Up and Leave Insecurity Behind* (New York: William Morrow, 2011).

Rahula, W., *What the Buddha Taught* (New York: Grove Press, 1959).

Raven, P. H., & Johnson, G. B., *Biology*, 5th Edition (Boston: McGraw-Hill, 1999).

Salzberg, S., *Lovingkindness: The Revolutionary Art of Happiness* (Boston: Shambhala Publications, 1995).

Segal, Z. V., Williams, J. M. G., & Teasdale, J. D., *Mindfulness-Based Cognitive Therapy for Depression: A New Approach to Preventing Relapse* (New York: Guilford Press, 2002).

Siegel, D. J., *The Developing Mind* (New York: Guilford Press, 1999).

Siegel, D. J., *The Mindful Brain* (New York: Norton, 2007).

Tirch, D., "Mindfulness as a Context for the Cultivation for Compassion," *International Journal of Cognitive Psychotherapy*, 3, (2010), 113–23.

Tirch, D. D., & Leahy, R. L., "Anxiety and Our Relationship to Emotional Experience: The Role of Emotional Schemas, Psychological Flexibility and Mindfulness." Paper presented at the International Congress of Cognitive Psychotherapy, Istanbul (June, 2011).

Tirch, D. D., Leahy, R. L., & Silberstein, L., "Relationships among Emotional Schemas, Psychological Flexibility, Dispositional Mindfulness, and Emotion Regulation." Paper presented at the meeting of the Association for Behavioral and Cognitive Therapies, New York (November, 2009).

Williams, M., Teasdale, J., Segal, Z., & Kabat-Zinn, J., *The Mindful Way through Depression* (New York: Guilford Press, 2007).

Wilson, D. S., & Wilson, E. O., "Rethinking the Theoretical Foundation of Sociobiology," *Quarterly Review of Biology*, 82(4), 327–48.

Wilson, K. G., & DuFrene, T., *Mindfulness for Two: An Acceptance and Commitment Therapy Approach to Mindfulness in Psychotherapy* (Oakland, CA: New Harbinger, 2009).

WEB

My own website has many links to resources on compassion, mindfulness, and acceptance, as well as audio exercises for the practices in this book.
mindfulcompassion.com

The Compassionate Mind Foundation is a wonderful resource for all of the great work going on in CFT.
compassionatemind.co.uk

The website of Kristin Neff, PhD, associate professor in human development and culture at the University of Texas at Austin, is another great resource for compassion-focused work.
self-compassion.org

Chris Germer, PhD, clinical psychologist, has a large variety of resources available at his website.
mindfulselfcompassion.org

Dennis D. Tirch, PhD, is associate director of the American Institute for Cognitive Therapy, founder and director of the Center for Mindfulness and Compassion-Focused Cognitive Behavioral Therapy, and serves as adjunct assistant clinical professor at Weill-Cornell Medical College. He is coauthor of books and articles on mindfulness, acceptance, and compassion, and maintains an active research program in these areas with Robert L. Leahy. Tirch is a fellow of the Academy of Cognitive Therapy and founding co-president of the New York City chapter of the Association for Contextual Behavioral Science.

Foreword writer **Paul Gilbert, PhD,** is a professor at the University of Derby in the United Kingdom, director of the mental health research unit at Derbyshire Mental Health Trust, founder of compassion-focused therapy, and author of *The Compassionate Mind.*